Elementary
Task Listening

Teacher's Book

Jacqueline St Clair Stokes

CAMBRIDGE
UNIVERSITY PRESS

PUBLISHED BY THE PRESS SYNDICATE OF THE UNIVERSITY OF CAMBRIDGE
The Pitt Building, Trumpington Street, Cambridge CB2 1RP, United Kingdom

CAMBRIDGE UNIVERSITY PRESS
The Edinburgh Building, Cambridge CB2 2RU, United Kingdom
40 West 20th Street, New York, NY 10011–4211, USA
10 Stamford Road, Oakleigh, Melbourne 3166, Australia

First published 1984
Eleventh printing 1997

Printed in the United Kingdom at the University Press, Cambridge

ISBN 0 521 27582 2 Teacher's Book
ISBN 0 521 27578 4 Student's Book
ISBN 0 521 25594 5 Cassette

A27125

Contents

Introduction

Elementary Task Listening consists of listening materials and thematically related reading and writing activities at an elementary level. Designed to be flexible, it can be used by students with fairly sophisticated reading and writing skills who lack exposure to authentic spoken English as well as by students who have only been learning English for a short time. It will also be found useful in preparing for task-based examinations in English as a Foreign Language, such as the Oxford Preliminary Examination and the RSA Examination in the Communicative Use of English as a Foreign Language.

There are twenty-one units in *Elementary Task Listening*. The basis for each unit is a short tape recording of unscripted English spoken at normal speed in a variety of situations. The topics have been chosen to aid the student whose goal is to use English in an international context: travel, sightseeing, business meetings and shopping are among the topics covered. A variety of accents (American, British, French, Japanese etc.) are also included to mirror the real-life use of English as an international language. Each recording is accompanied by a task which is designed to encourage the development of a particular listening skill, such as listening to a recorded announcement for specific details, overhearing a conversation and sifting out the relevant information, following a set of instructions, listening for the gist of a conversation. Follow-up reading and writing tasks which share the same theme are provided for each unit.

The purpose of all the tasks is to aid comprehension. Students should aim to complete the task, not to understand every word on the tape. The tasks often involve using the kind of forms, charts, diagrams, lists and maps which occur in real life. They can easily be adapted to suit the ability of the class or individual student.

Each unit features many of the language functions, structures and lexical items found in elementary course books, and certain key items, such as suggestions, directions, dates and times reappear in different units throughout *Elementary Task Listening*.

The units are not arranged in any particular order of difficulty. However, students will find those units which occur towards the beginning of the book are generally shorter or more straightforward than later ones. Reference to the Teacher's Book and cassette will help determine the order which best suits your students.

Teacher's Book

The Teacher's Book contains objectives, information about the recording, teaching procedures and completed task pages for each unit.

The objectives briefly describe the goals for the listening, reading and writing activities. They provide a useful quick reference system for the teacher looking for follow-up material. For example, work done in class on numbers and money might be reinforced by Unit 2, where one objective is 'to give students practice in listening to expressions of quantity and cost'.

For each unit, the information about the tape recording includes the tapescript and details of the length, number of speakers, accents and setting. The tapescript indicates where overlapping speech and hesitations occur, but their effect on the level of difficulty is best judged by listening to the tape. Recordings usually have two speakers and last between one and three minutes. A wide variety of voices and accents have been used. The recordings of speakers with non-British accents are not necessarily the most difficult. Care has been taken to ensure that the key information for task completion is not masked by the accent. In Unit 7, for example, a Japanese and a British secretary arrange a business meeting; the details which are needed to complete the task are clearly conveyed by the British secretary. Unit 12 is the one exception: here English is used as a lingua franca by two non-English speakers.

The *Key language* section contains the language items from the tapescript which are relevant to completion of the listening task. It is divided into *Lexis* and *Structures*. An item is normally listed under *Structures* if it is possible to make substitutions within the phrase. Fixed expressions such as 'You're welcome' and 'Have a nice day!' are included in *Lexis* and should be taught as one-off vocabulary items.

All the teaching procedures emphasize the importance of making full use of students' knowledge and experience. Suggestions are made to encourage students to use their predictive and deductive skills when dealing with the material. The ideas, examples and procedures included in the teacher's notes are by no means exhaustive, nor will they suit all students. The material should be used in the way which best suits specific students' needs.

The teaching procedure is divided into four sections: *Before listening*, *Listening task*, *Reading task* and *Writing task*. *Before listening* provides a number of ideas for practising the key language and introducing the listening task. These preliminary activities can be used in preceding lessons or immediately before listening.

The procedure suggested under *Listening task* normally involves three steps: setting the scene, making clear what information is to be listened for and playing the tape (as many times as is necessary) for students to complete the task. Some ways to simplify the task are also included for students who are obviously having difficulties, and some extension activities suggested for students who find the main task easy.

The *Reading task* and *Writing task* sections also contain suggested teaching procedures.

The completed task pages reproduce the Student's Book pages, with the answers filled in. In some cases these will only be suggested possible answers.

1   Changing travellers cheques

OBJECTIVES

1 To give students practice in following a simple financial exchange in a bank.
2 To give students practice in recording information relating to date, rates and amounts.
3 To help students sift out and record the advantages and disadvantages of a variety of ways to take money abroad.

RECORDING

Tapescript

Length: 1 min.
Number of speakers: 2 (1 American).
Setting: In a bank.

Clerk: Good afternoon, sir. Can I help you?
Customer: Yes I hope so. Erm, can I change travellers cheques here?
Clerk: Certainly. Could I have some means of identification?
Customer: Oh, er, well, I've got a driver's license or er a passport.
Clerk: Oh, a passport will be fine.
Customer: Ah, there you go.
Clerk: How many cheques would you like to change?
Customer: Erm, two of the fifty dollar ones. (Mm-mm). Oh, what's the exchange rate?
Clerk: The exchange rate? Oh, today it's a dollar sixty-four to the pound.
Customer: Mm-mm.
Clerk: Now for $100 that will be ... yes ... erm ... £60.98.
Customer: Fine. What's the date today?

Clerk: Er, thirty-first of August.
Customer: Thirty-first of August. There you go.
Clerk: Oh, er, you have to sign both the cheques.
Customer: Ah!
Clerk: Mm-mm. Er, how would you like the money, sir?
Customer: Six tens.
Clerk: Six tens. That's ten, twenty, thirty, forty, fifty, sixty, ninety-eight.
Customer: Ah. Thanks a lot. Bye.
Clerk: Thank you. Goodbye.

Key language

Function: Asking for and giving information about date, rates and amounts.

Lexis: travellers cheques   dollar
               identification   pound (pence)
               driver's license (US)   date
               passport   to sign
               to change (cheques)   both (the cheques)
               (a) fifty dollar one   tens (*denomination*)
               exchange rate

Structures: Can I change ...?
                  How many ...?
                  ($1.64) to the pound
                  for ($100) that will be ...
                  What's the date today?
                  The (thirty-first) of (August)
                  How would you like the money?

PROCEDURE

Before listening

Begin this unit by bringing to the session an assortment of foreign currency. Divide the class into two teams and have a quiz to see how many of the coins and notes can be identified. This could lead into a discussion of how much each is worth. Students who have recently travelled abroad will probably remember something about the exchange rate they got on their holiday.

Prepare a worksheet to guide practice of the key language. Include details of simple role plays in which money is changed from one currency to another: e.g. an American wants to change $100 into the local currency; students work in pairs and one plays the American and the other the bank clerk. A list of exchange rates can be obtained from a bank or the newspaper. Make sure students are familiar with the symbols for the various currencies, e.g. £(pound), $(dollar), and that they can write the exchange rate, e.g. $1.64 = £1.

A question about the preferred denominations is included on the tape but is not part of the listening task. If your students can cope easily with the listening, you may wish to spend time on this aspect. Practise the question 'How would you like the money?' and possible responses.

Check that everyone knows the months of the year and their abbreviated written forms: i.e. Jan., Feb., March, April, May, June, July, Aug., Sept., Oct., Nov., Dec. Show how the date can be expressed using numbers: e.g. 31/8/84 (day, month, year). You should also point out that an American would write this: 8/31/84 (month, day, year).

Ask students whether they have used travellers cheques before. Those who have can tell others the procedure for changing them. Make sure they mention where they can be changed and the identification needed.

Open the Student's Book to page 2 and look at the customer's record of purchase. Explain that this accompanies the travellers cheques supplied by many companies. Someone may suggest the purpose of the record.

Tell the students that the owner of these cheques is American and is going to change some of them in England. Encourage students to tell you the information they are going to be listening for – number of cheques changed, date, exchange rate and amount received.

Listening task

Play the tape as many times as is necessary for the students to fill in the missing information. The task can be simplified by asking them to listen for only one piece of information at a time: first of all the number of cheques changed (2 × $50), then the date (31st August), the exchange rate ($1.64 to the pound), and finally, the amount received (£60.98).

The sheer volume of numbers mentioned may cause confusion, so allow sufficient time before playing the tape for predicting the frame and content.

For students who manage this task easily, ask them to listen for three further details: first, the expression the American uses when he hands over his passport and later his cheques to the bank clerk: 'There you go'. Students may guess the meaning of the phrase and also suggest the British equivalent: 'There you are'. Second, the American repeats the date. The purpose is not to check the information. What is he doing at this point? Third, the clerk tells him to sign both cheques. Why? Had he forgotten to sign one of them or the two?

Reading task

The article is similar to those appearing in magazines and holiday brochures. The task is to read it and sort out the relative advantages and disadvantages of the three ways of taking money abroad.

Ask students to read the article and underline words and phrases they do not understand. Let them try to work out possible explanations for the parts underlined, using clues from the context. 'Refund' may cause difficulties and this may be the time to do some vocabulary building, focussing on how parts of the word give clues to its meaning. In this case '*Re-*' as a prefix meaning 'again' as in '*re*play', '*re*do'.

Ask students to find the advantages of taking travellers cheques abroad and to indicate these with a tick in the margin. Ask them to indicate disadvantages with a cross in the margin. Repeat for cash and credit cards. Encourage students to tell anecdotes about their experiences with foreign currencies.

Writing task

Students record the advantages and disadvantages in the space provided. Only brief notes are necessary to complete this part successfully.

COMPLETED LISTENING TASK

1 Changing travellers cheques

Fill in the missing information.

Customer's record of purchase

List full serial number of each cheque. When used record here.

CHEQUE AMOUNT	SERIAL NUMBER	DATE USED	EXCHANGE RATE	AMOUNT RECEIVED
$50	FB 100 - 830 - 78	31 Aug	£1 = $1·64	} £60·98
$50	FB 100 - 830 - 79	31 Aug	"	
$50	FB 100 - 830 - 80			
$50	FB 100 - 830 - 81			
$50	FB 100 - 830 - 82			
$20	FB 100 - 830 - 83			
$20	FB 100 - 830 - 84			

CARRY THIS RECORD SEPARATELY FROM TRAVELLERS CHEQUES

COMPLETED WRITING TASK

Practical information and advice to make your holiday a success

TRAVELLERS CHEQUES

If stolen, tell the police and visit the nearest refund agency. You'll then get a full or partial refund immediately. Keep a list of cheque numbers and a note of those already cashed, and don't carry this with the cheques themselves.

MONEY

CASH

Taking only cash is a risk. If you lose it, you can't get a refund! You may find the exchange rate for cash is not as good as for travellers cheques.

CREDIT CARDS

The best way to buy things abroad is by credit card, because you don't have to pay until you get home.

The exchange rates used by credit companies are usually very good for their customers.

If you would like to receive full booking details of a subscription scheme, please fill in this ... and send it to the ...
(Please tick box)

Note the advantages and disadvantages
of the three ways of taking money abroad.

	Advantages	Disadvantages
Travellers cheques	If stolen, full or partial refund immediately.	
Cash		If you lose it, you can't get a refund. Exchange rates may not be as good as for travellers cheques.
Credit cards	Don't have to pay until you get home. Exchange rates usually very good.	

3

2   Sending mail

OBJECTIVES

1 To help students follow a typical exchange in a post office.
2 To give students practice in listening to expressions of quantity and cost.
3 To give students an idea of the price of goods in the UK and to help them compare these with prices in their own country.

RECORDING

Tapescript

Length: 1 min. 10 sec.
Number of speakers: 2 (1 American).
Setting: In a post office.

Customer: Hello. I have er three letters I'd like to send to the States.
Post office assistant: Right. That's twenty-er ... six pence each if they are not above 26 grams.
Customer: OK. What's the price of er ... post-cards?
Assistant: By airmail, twenty-four pence.
Customer: And the price of airmail letters?
Assistant: That's twenty-four pence and it's no difference in price if it's for the States or anywhere else.
Customer: OK. Well I'd like stamps to send the three letters and five postcards and two airmail letters.

Assistant: Right, so the letters that's twenty-six pence, three letters that's seventy-eight pence. And the five postcards at twenty-four pence that's £1.20. And the two airmail letters at twenty-four pence that's forty-eight pence. That's £2.46 altogether, please.
Customer: Here you are. Here's £3.
Assistant: Right and fifty-four pence change. Thank you.
Customer: Thank you.

Key language

Function: Asking for and giving information about quantity and cost.

Lexis:

letter	postcard
to send	by airmail
the States	airmail letter
price	stamp

change	twenty-four pence
Here you are	£1.20 (one pound twenty (pence))
numbers 1–100	£3 (three pounds)

Structures: I'd like to ...
That's ... each/altogether.
What's the price of ...?
I'd like the ... / a ... / ...s
(Five postcards) at (24 pence) that's (£1.20).

PROCEDURE

Before listening

Students should be familiar with numbers and British money. This topic is often covered early in elementary courses. It is a more difficult task to recognise numbers when they occur embedded in a conversation than in isolation, so this listening unit will be a good follow-up activity.

Almost everyone who goes on holiday sends postcards home. So most of us have bought stamps using a mixture of gesture and the odd word. Help students piece together a dialogue frame for buying stamps in English. Someone may ask about different rates for different types of mail; if not, open the Student's Book to page 4 and identify the mail shown there. Point out the abbreviation for pence is 'p'. Ask students to suggest why the aerogramme or airmail letter already has a stamp.

Listening task

This unit occurs early in *Elementary Task Listening* because it is a good one to use to introduce students to listening to unscripted English. The pre-listening teaching is important to ensure students can complete the task successfully and rapidly.

Play the tape, and ask simple questions, e.g. 'How many people were talking?' 'How many men?' 'What were they doing?' 'Who was buying/ selling?' 'Were they both English?' The aim of your questioning is to set the scene for the listening. Now, if you have not already done so, get students to open the Student's Book to page 4 and look at the three pieces of mail. Tell them to listen again and to note the cost of sending a letter, a postcard and an airmail letter to the States. Finally, ask them to note the number of pieces of mail the American is sending and to calculate the total cost. Play the tape as many times as necessary, but try to move things along so that it does not become laborious.

Note: The cost of sending these pieces of mail was correct at the time of recording the cassette. Please warn students that since then prices have risen!

Reading task

The aim of this part of the unit is to get an idea of the price of everyday goods and services in the UK. Obviously there is a range of prices and these increase from year to year.

Let students look at page 5 in their books. The list of prices with the film may need some explanation. The prices are for the cost of developing and printing, not for buying the film. Help students deduce the meaning of the abbreviations 'No.', 'exps.', etc.

Writing task

Find the present exchange rate of the local currency to the pound. Ask students to estimate the cost of the goods and services displayed. Use the exchange rate to convert the UK prices. Now prices in the UK and at home can be compared.

If your students come from a variety of countries, ask them to do the calculations individually. Students can then report their comparisons to the class. This should provide a good deal of oral practice of some of the key language as well as the language of comparison. If students find this an interesting topic, they may want to make comparisons with other countries. Perhaps you could set the task of finding out the cheapest place to obtain each of these goods. Someone is sure to notice that quality does not come into these comparisons!

2 Sending mail

Put the correct postage on each piece of mail. Fill in the calculation below.

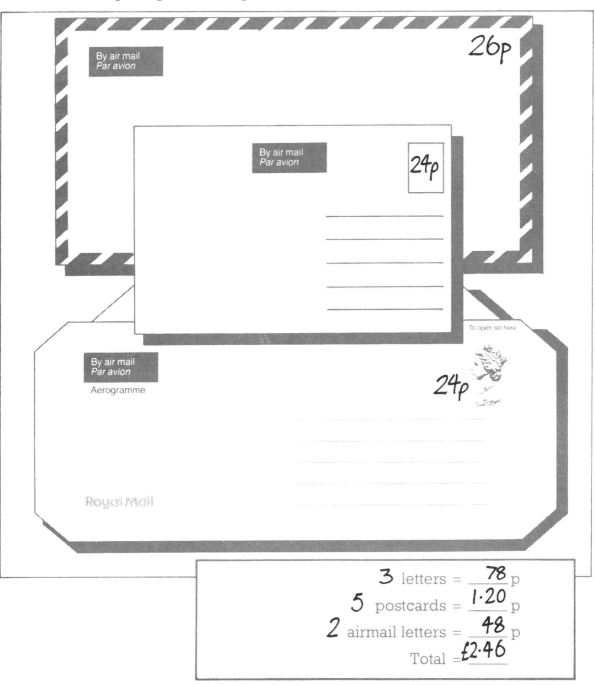

By air mail
Par avion

26p

By air mail
Par avion

24p

To open slit here

By air mail
Par avion

Aerogramme

24p

Royal Mail

3 letters =	78	p
5 postcards =	1·20	p
2 airmail letters =	48	p
Total =	£2·46	

Developing and printing

NO. OF EXPS. ON FILM	PRICE
12	1·55
20	1·95
24	2·25
36	2·95

5p — 10p

£1.25 — £5.00

Car parking rates

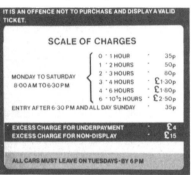

IT IS AN OFFENCE NOT TO PURCHASE AND DISPLAY A VALID TICKET.

SCALE OF CHARGES

	0 - 1 HOUR	35p
	1 - 2 HOURS	50p
	2 - 3 HOURS	80p
MONDAY TO SATURDAY	3 - 4 HOURS	£1·30p
8·00 AM TO 6·30 PM	4 - 6 HOURS	£1·80p
	6 - 10½ HOURS	£2·50p
ENTRY AFTER 6·30 PM AND ALL DAY SUNDAY		35p

EXCESS CHARGE FOR UNDERPAYMENT	£4
EXCESS CHARGE FOR NON-DISPLAY	£15

ALL CARS MUST LEAVE ON TUESDAYS - BY 6 PM

Double beefburger and chips
£2.10

15p — 30p

What is the exchange rate for your money? £1 = 11·37 French francs.
Write down how much these items cost in the UK, in your money.
Write down how much they cost in your country.
Which items are more expensive to buy in the UK? Which items are cheaper in the UK? Put a tick in the appropriate column.

Item	Price in the UK	Price at home	more expensive	cheaper
Film developing (24, colour)	25·50 Ffr	90 Ffr		✓
Telephone call	·50 — 1 Ffr	1 Ffr		✓
Paperback	14 - 57 Ffr	15 - 50 Ffr	Same	
Parking for 1 hour	4 Ffr	5 Ffr		✓
Beefburger and chips	24 Ffr	14 Ffr	✓	
Newspaper	1·70 - 3·50 Ffr	4 - 4·50 Ffr		✓

3 Coming through immigration

OBJECTIVES

---

1 To help students prepare for travelling to an English-speaking country.
2 To give students practice in asking someone about their plans.
3 To acquaint students with some import regulations.
4 To give students practice in filling out a landing card.

RECORDING

Tapescript

Length: 1 min. 12 sec.
Number of speakers: 2 (1 American).
Setting: Immigration control at Boston airport.

Immigration inspector: Welcome to Boston. May I see your passport? ... Oh I see you've been here before.
Visitor: Hm-mm, a couple of times.
Inspector: Hm-mm. Er what's the purpose of your visit?
Visitor: Erm, it's a holiday.
Inspector: Hm-mm. Where are you going to go?
Visitor: Erm, erm I'm going from here to Atlanta, then, then across to California and erm then I'm going to the Mid-West and erm and, and then back to Boston.
Inspector: Hm-mm. Where are you going to stay?

Visitor: Er, well mainly with friends.
Inspector: Hm-mm. And how long are you going to be here?
Visitor: Well, I ... about three months or, or until the money runs out.
Inspector: Hm-mm. Erm, what's the date of your return?
Visitor: I, I've got an open ticket.
Inspector: OK then I'll ... erm ... make it February 22nd.
Visitor: Thanks.
Inspector: Thank you. Have a nice day!

Key language

Function: Enquiring about someone's plans.

Lexis:		
	Welcome to ...	friend
	passport	about (three months)
	a couple of (times)	money
	visit	to run out
	holiday	open ticket
	to stay	Have a nice day!

Structures: May I see ...?
What's the purpose of your visit / date of your return?
Where ⎪ are you going to ...?
How long ⎪
I'm going to ..., then to ..., then back to ...
... or until ...

PROCEDURE

Before listening

Encourage students to talk about their intentions for travelling in the future as a way to practise the key language. The variety of ways of talking about future plans in English can cause headaches! Use this opportunity to practise two ways of expressing future plans. The 'going to' form can be used to talk about plans for the near future, e.g. 'I'm going to watch television this evening', and for the distant future, e.g. 'I'm going to make a million someday'. This will avoid the common misconception among students that 'will' is for the distant future and 'going to' for the near future.

There is, however a distinction to be made between these two forms which relates to the time of speaking. Use the 'going to' form to talk about plans made *prior to* the time of speaking and the 'will' form for plans made *at* the time of speaking.

Students who have travelled extensively will be able to give an account of the stages passengers pass through when leaving their country and entering another, e.g. check luggage, go through passport control.

Ask everyone to make a note of the questions they might be asked by a foreign immigration inspector. Make a list of these on the board. Compare these with the list on page 6 in the Student's Book. Students may notice that some of these questions are more likely to be asked by a customs officer.

Listening task

Ask students to look at the photographs on page 6 in the Student's Book and guess the country. Tell them they are going to hear a woman at passport control in Boston. They have to listen to the questions the immigration inspector asks and indicate these by ticking the corresponding question on the list in their books. Finally, questions can be asked about the woman's plans, but there is only limited value in asking students to note the details of someone else's trip. Instead, ask students to plan their own trip to the States. Provide maps and information about the States. Use these details in role playing as a follow-up to the listening.

Reading task

Many students who have travelled abroad will be familiar with the notion of Duty and Tax Free Allowances. For these students, you only have to provide the language to describe the allowance system. Do this by asking questions about how they spend their time in airports between checking in and flying out.

Some students will have had no experience of international travel, so be prepared to explain the allowance system. Basically, it allows travellers to bring into the country small quantities of such goods as tobacco and alcohol which have been purchased free of duty and tax. The crucial question is how much each person can import before duty has to be paid. In Britain this depends on where the goods were bought and whether European tax and duty have been paid.

Make full use of your students' experience of travelling to establish the context for the reading task. The excerpt from a customs information leaflet on page 7 in the Student's Book is complex. How you handle it depends on the level of your students. For the most elementary students, exposure to this kind of written material is the goal, while more advanced students can be expected to manipulate the information. Ask students to look at the excerpt and tell them that this applies to travellers arriving in the United Kingdom. Draw their attention to the difference between columns 1 and 2. Check comprehension of key language items, e.g. weights and volumes. Ask simple questions to aid comprehension of the most important information, namely: (1) there are limits on the amount of goods that can be brought into the country; (2) the limits vary according to where the goods were bought, where the traveller is from and how long the traveller intends to stay.

Prepare a worksheet of situations for your more advanced students. On the worksheet, outline a number of profiles of the following type: 'A sixteen-year-old boy is travelling alone to England and wants to buy some duty-free cigarettes and perfume. What is he allowed to import?'

Writing task

Travellers to Britain are required to fill in a landing card and present it at passport control. The card is reproduced with the French and Spanish translation as it occurs in the original. Most of the forms your students will ever have to fill out in English will include this kind of question. Make sure 'Block Capitals' and the format for recording date of birth (day, month, year) are understood.

COMPLETED LISTENING TASK

3 Coming through immigration

Tick the questions that the immigration inspector asked.

✓	May I see your passport?
	Where are you from?
	What do you do?
	Are you travelling alone?
	Do you have anything to declare?
	Have you been here before?
✓	What's the purpose of your visit?
✓	How long are you going to be here?
	Where is your luggage?
✓	What is the date of your return?
✓	Where are you going to go?
	Do you intend working here?
✓	Where are you going to stay?
	Have you enough money for your visit?

sweater	to read
shirt	That's right
underneath	to work
glasses	library

Structures: the one/Steve with ...
You'll never guess ...
He is tall/fat.
Does he have a beard/moustache?
He has a beard/moustache.
He always wears ...
Does he wear ...?

PROCEDURE

Before listening

Use the photographs on page 8 in the Student's Book to introduce or revise the key language. Practise asking about appearances by getting students to take turns to pick one photograph and having the rest of the class ask questions to guess the chosen photograph. Further practice can be gained by having students think of someone well-known to the class and describing his appearance and occupation. If your students have a hard time thinking of people, have some cards with names and details available. Miming can also be a fun way of working on this language area. Students call out the description as it is acted and you can indicate the correct response. In this way a lot of practice can be done in a short time while interest is high.

Set the scene for the listening by asking the students to tell you about anything unusual that has happened to them on a train. You may have a story to tell yourself. Tell them that the episode from the train journey they are going to hear was eventful only because Helen and Bart met an old friend of theirs, Steve.

Listening task

The task is to identify Steve from among the photographs on page 8 in the Student's Book. Steve's picture should be marked with a tick. If students find this very easy, ask them to list the key facts which brought them to their decision.

Reading task

Ask students to read the *Penfriend Wanted* advertisement on page 9 in their books. This kind of advertisement is occasionally found in English Language

Teaching magazines. Writing to a penfriend in English is certainly a good way to practise the language.

Find Thailand and Bangkok in an atlas. Ask your students to suggest the kinds of questions they would like to ask Boonyarit if they met him. Encourage them to think about the kind of thing Boonyarit would like to know about them. Help them to plan a reply to Boonyarit's letter.

Writing task

A parallel reply to Boonyarit's letter can be easily constructed by changing the details. If your students have a better command of written English, this could be a freer writing activity.

If students find the idea of writing to a penfriend in English interesting, you could write to a school in another country and try to interest them in the idea.

4 Describing someone

Put a tick in the box beside the photograph of Steve.

COMPLETED WRITING TASK

This letter appeared in an English Language Teaching magazine. Read it and then write your reply to Boonyarit.

NOTICEBOARD

Contacts and exchanges

BRITISH GRAMMAR SCHOOL

PENFRIEND WANTED

I am a Thai student and I want a penfriend so I can practise my English. I study English and law. I want to study in America later. I am going to be a lawyer. I am short and a bit thin. I have short, black, straight hair and dark brown eyes. I have three brothers and a sister.

I like going to the cinema and listening to music. I also like travelling. I went to Australia a year ago.

If you want to be my penfriend please tell me all about yourself. I look forward to hearing from you.

Boonyarit Phongmekin
P.O. Box 1019, Bangkok, Thailand.

Events

To have a meeting listed in the Practical English Teaching 'Events' column, send details to the Editor, 140 Kensington Church Street, London W8 4BN at least three months in advance.

IATEFL (International Association of Teachers of English as a Foreign Language)
April 25-27 1984, Gröningen, The Netherlands

Amsterdam 100-404
Guadalajara,
Jalisco.
Mexico 45700
June 10, 1984

Dear Boonyarit,

I was pleased to read your letter in a magazine at school. I am looking for a penfriend too!

I work for an importing company during the day and I study English at night school. I am 18. I have short black hair and brown eyes. I have a brother and a sister. I like going to the beach, listening to music and dancing. I like travelling too. I went to Spain and Portugal last year.

If you want to be my penfriend please write back soon and send a photograph.

Best wishes,
Patricia Noriega.

5 Checking flight departure time

OBJECTIVES

1 To give students practice in listening to airline recorded information and sifting out details relevant to a specific flight.
2 To give students practice in talking about dates and times and recording this information in written form.

RECORDING

Tapescript

Length: 1 min 50 sec.
Number of speakers: 1.
Setting: A telephone recorded message.

... 20·35.
Departures
Air Canada eight one five to Calgary and Vancouver departing at 15·30. Qantas Airways QF oh one eight, oh one six and zero zero eight to Bahrain, Kuala Lumpur, Singapore, Perth, Brisbane and Sydney departing at 19·35. Any changes to flight arrivals or departures will be recorded immediately. Thank you.

This is an Air Canada and Qantas Airways recorded announcement. The following flights will arrive and depart from Heathrow London on Sunday the seventh of November.

Arrivals
All flights for today have arrived except Air Canada eight five eight from Toronto which is arriving at 20·35.
Departures
Air Canada eight one five to Calgary and Vancouver departing at 15·30. Qantas Airways QF oh one eight, oh one six and zero zero eight to Bahrain, Kuala Lumpur, Singapore, Perth, Brisbane and Sydney departing at 19·35. Any changes to flight arrivals or departures will be recorded immediately. Thank you.

Key language

Function: Giving information about flight arrivals and departures.

Lexis:
departure	arrival
Air Canada 815	recorded announcement
Qantas airways	Heathrow London
flight	

Structures: departing/arriving at ... (*time*)
                            ... will arrive (at) ... (*place*) and depart from ... (*place*)
                            on ... (*day*)

PROCEDURE

Before listening

Help students anticipate the content of the tape by asking questions about the sequence of events prior to flying, e.g. book flight, pack bags, check flight departure time. Some of your students will have had experience of flying and so suggestions should come from them. Your questions can direct the conversation so the key lexis will be covered.

This is also a good time to revise work done on prepositions of time (*at* 15.30, *on* Sunday) and place (*in* Calgary, *at* Singapore airport). Depending on the abilities of your students, revision of numbers as in Air Canada 815, and the twenty-four hour clock may also be required. 'Bingo' is a fun way of revising the twenty-four hour clock. Write twenty times on the board, e.g. 15.30, 9.35. Practise these orally. Each student then draws a grid consisting of three boxes across and three down and fills the nine boxes with times from the board. Call out the times randomly and the student whose nine are called first wins. This can be repeated with the student who won calling out times.

Make sure everyone has understood the purpose of a recorded airline announcement, i.e. it gives information about flight arrivals and departures. Look at the ticket on page 10 in the Student's Book. Ask students to tell you the information they can get from the ticket – date, flight number, airline, destination. Identify the missing piece of information, i.e. the flight departure time. This is the specific information students have to listen for to complete the ticket.

Use an atlas to locate Singapore. Talk about the duration of the flight, whether it will stop anywhere en route, where it will go after Singapore, etc.

The purpose of the pre-listening stage is to help students predict *the form* of the message, i.e. there will be information about arrivals and departures and *the content* i.e. there will be airline flight numbers and places mentioned. Examination of the ticket tells the students which piece of information they are going to listen for, i.e. the departure time of one specific flight to one specific destination. Discussion of the flight as suggested alerts the students to the fact that the place name may be embedded.

Listening task

Play the tape and let students fill in the departure time. This may require repeated listening. The tape does not begin at the beginning of the recorded annnouncement and this adds to its difficulty.

Reading task

This will serve to reinforce the work done prior to listening. Students should be able to deduce the meaning of 'flight itinerary'. Draw students' attention to the upper half of the itinerary and do not get embroiled in the notes about reconfirming (these have been included for the sake of authenticity). Use an atlas to locate the cities. The itinerary can be used for oral practice of the key structures if desired. Discussion of distances and flying times may lead you into considering time zones. If more work is needed on time, this may be an interesting route to take.

Writing task

When the reading has been completed, students simply read the letter and fill in the missing information. Remind them that the preposition preceding the space can help determine whether a time, day or place should be inserted.

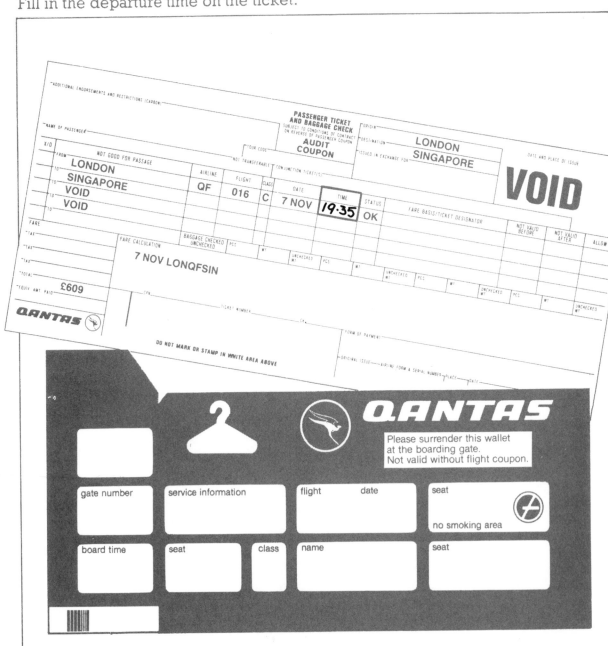

COMPLETED LISTENING TASK

5 Checking flight departure time

Fill in the departure time on the ticket.

COMPLETED WRITING TASK

Using the information from the flight itinerary,
complete the letter to Mr and Mrs Rodway.

A. Levine Travel Bureau Ltd.

FLIGHT ITINERARY

FROM	TO	CLASS	FLIGHT	DATE	DEP.	ARR.
Montreal	Toronto		CP 183	Apr. 30	11:55AM	1:00PM
Toronto	Vancouver		CP 161	Apr. 30	4:45PM	8:30PM
Vancouver	Portland		WA 456	May 2	5:45PM	6:37PM
		Have a pleasant trip				

Please reconfirm — North American onward flights at least 6 hours before departure. Overseas flights at least 72 hours before departure.
Times shown above are based on current timetables and are subject to change without notice.   ALWAYS RECONFIRM

113 Peel St.
Montreal H3V 1A8
April 2nd 1984

Dear Mr. and Mrs. Rodway,

I received the times of my flights this morning. I fly to Vancouver via Toronto on _April 30th_. I have to wait nearly four hours in _Toronto_ airport! I spend two days in _Vancouver_ and then arrive in Portland on _May 2nd_ at _6·37p.m._ I'm looking forward to seeing you.

Best wishes,
Sylvie Thibodeau

11

6 Reserving hotel accommodation

OBJECTIVES

---

1 To give students practice in listening to someone arranging overnight accommodation.
2 To give students practice in reading authentic American advertising material related to hotel accommodation.
3 To help students prepare questions for arranging accommodation for themselves.

RECORDING

Tapescript

Length: 1 min 33 sec.
Number of speakers: 2 (1 American).
Setting: At a hotel reservations desk in an American airport.

Clerk: Yes sir. Can I help you?
Traveller: Yes, I wonder if you can. I need a hotel room.
Clerk: Er, how long will that be for?
Traveller: Er, just the one night.
Clerk: Ah-huh. Well we've got the er Park Hotel which is $75 a night, er and there are some vacancies at the Skyline Hotel which is $70 a night.
Traveller: Yes. Are they both near the centre?
Clerk: Ah, well. The Skyline is near er the airport, which is er is good if you have to catch an early flight and the Park is downtown which is er, you know, near restaurants er night-clubs and shows, things like that. Erm ... what time is your flight out?
Traveller: Oh I'm not going till midday. I ... I think I'll erm ... I think I'll go to the Park actually. I can see a show tonight.
Clerk: Er. OK. Er, shall I make you a reservation for tonight?

Traveller: Oh, well if you can, yes, that would be most kind of you.
Clerk: Right so er let me just get the details now. That's a single room, er, for tonight and er your name please?
Traveller: Er, Mr Garland, John Garland.
Clerk: John Garland. Right, just a minute Mr Garland. (*Dials hotel*) Er, hello, yes. I'd like to make a reservation for a single room, for tonight, March 1st, and the name is erm Mr John Garland. Thank you. Well that's confirmed Mr Garland.
Traveller: Ah, it's most kind of you. Oh, er, how do I get there?
Clerk: Ah, well you take the shuttle bus and that comes every fifteen minutes. Er now it leaves from the bus stop outside the main airport doors, over there on your left.
Traveller: Many thanks. Thank you.
Clerk: Right! You're welcome.

Key language

Function: Arranging accommodation.

Lexis:
hotel room	night-club
one night	show
($75) a night	details
near	single room
centre	tonight
airport	just a minute
early flight	shuttle bus
downtown	bus stop
restaurant	You're welcome

Structures: Can I help you?
How long for?
Your (name), please?
I'd like to make a reservation ...
It comes every (fifteen) minutes.
It leaves from ...

PROCEDURE

Before listening

To practise the key language new to students or in need of revision, let the class plan a trip abroad. Compile a list of things to be arranged on the board: transport to airport, flight, hotel. Divide the class into groups. Give each group one of these headings and ask them to investigate the options and present these to the class. Provide the required information in the form of brochures and timetables. Make sure the amount of information you provide is suitable for the level of the class. This may mean you have to reduce brochures to a few key facts and transfer these to handwritten cards.

Ask students whether they have ever flown to the States. Use a map to locate the places they have visited. Tell them that at some of the large American airports there is often a desk marked 'Hotel Reservation Service'. Ask them to tell you the meaning of the sign and when travellers might use this service. Make it clear that this desk is at the airport and not in the hotel itself. The advantage of the service is that it is in contact with a number of hotels in the area and so saves the visitor the effort of phoning around to find a room.

Tell students they are going to hear a traveller, John Garland, talking to the assistant at the desk. Help them to predict the content of the conversation. Together, make a list of the information John Garland needs to choose a hotel (cost, access to downtown/airport). List the information the clerk needs to make a reservation for Mr Garland (length of stay, type of room).

Listening task

Tell students to listen for the names of the hotels mentioned. Play the tape. Now open the Student's Book to page 12 and look at the two invoices. Check these for unknown vocabulary. Play the tape again for students to determine which hotel John Garland chose. Ask students to fill in the seven pieces of missing information on the Park Hotel invoice. Finally they can complete the Skyline Hotel invoice. Ask which hotel they would have chosen and why.

Reading and writing tasks

Tell students that the reading piece comes from an authentic, American advertising brochure. If the preparation for the listening was adequate, students should have little trouble following the brochure and completing the writing task. If further practice is required before writing, have students decide on the questions to be asked orally and do the writing for homework.

6 Reserving hotel accommodation

Which hotel did John Garland choose? Fill in the correct invoice.
Fill in the missing information on the other invoice.

Skyline Hotel

225 UNION SQUARE, BOSTON
Close to AIRPORT

WELCOME

CHECK OUT HOUR 2 P.M.

ROOM	NAME	RATE	NO. NIGHTS	NO. PERSONS
312		$70		

FOR YOUR CONVENIENCE	SHUTTLE BUS SERVICE TO AIRPORT EVERY 5 MINUTES	ICE & SOFT DRINKS ON EACH FLOOR BY ELEVATOR

NAME JOHN GARLAND

DATE MARCH 1ST 19

00379

PARK HOTEL

335 Powell St. Boston
Close to DOWNTOWN

ROOM NO	RATE	NO. NIGHTS	NO. PERSONS	AMOUNT DUE
509	$75	1	1	

THANK YOU FOR STAYING AT THE

PARK HOTEL

WE HOPE YOU HAD A MOST ENJOYABLE STAY WITH US.

Shuttle bus service to airport every 15 minutes from outside hotel.

COMPLETED WRITING TASK

You are going to arrange hotel accommodation for you and your family at the hotel reservations counter. Think about the following details: position, single/double rooms, number of nights' stay, cost, transportation. Note the questions to ask.

Questions

1. Is there a hotel near the airport?

2. Can our 2 small children share our room?

3. How much is a double room for one night? Children extra?

4. How can we get to the hotel from the airport?

Need Hotel Accommodations in Boston or Anywhere in the USA?

Use Meegan's Free Hotel Reservations Service

When you arrive at the International Arrivals Building at Logan Airport, look for the Hotel Reservations counter outside of Customs. We'll be pleased to take care of all your hotel reservations needs at no cost to you.

Meegan Hotel Reservations Service provides a free, **convenient, personalized hotel reservations service.**

Our multi-lingual agents can:

- get you comfortable hotel accommodations in major area hotels at the price you want,

- provide you with detailed maps showing hotel locations in Boston, and advise you of the best transportation to use to get to your hotel, or to your final destination.

Meegan Hotel Reservations Service is part of an international hotel reservations service, paid for by area hotels.

Open seven days a week. Stop by or call:

(617) 569-3800

7 Arranging a business meeting

OBJECTIVES

1 To give students practice in following a secretary arranging a meeting over the phone.
2 To help students sift out the essential information from the conversation.
3 To give students practice in reading a variety of messages and using these to construct another message.

RECORDING

Tapescript

Length: 2 min. 24 sec.
Number of speakers: 2 (1 Japanese).
Setting: On the phone.

Mr Martin's secretary: Hello. Could I speak to Mr Seshimo's secretary please?
Mr Seshimo's secretary: Yes it is ... It's Mr Seshimo's secretary speaking.
Mr M.'s secretary: Oh hello. This is Martin Services in London.
Mr S.'s secretary: What can I do for you?
Mr M.'s secretary: Oh hello. Well my boss Mr Martin is coming out to Tokyo in the first week of December and I wanted to check that you knew he was coming.
Mr S.'s secretary: I did already know about it.
Mr M.'s secretary: Oh good.
Mr S.'s secretary: Er, he's coming for the conference.
Mr M.'s secretary: That's right yes, he's coming up for the conference erm ... and he would really like to take up Mr Seshimo's offer ... (Uh-huh) to visit the factory.
Mr S.'s secretary: Uh-huh. When would it be ... suit you? Er the conference er will be running from Tuesday to Thursday.
Mr M.'s secretary: Yes that's right. Tuesday to Thursday. Erm, well, either the Monday

or the Friday would be good. Which would be better for Mr Seshimo do you think?
Mr S.'s secretary: Er, as far as he's concerned the Monday will be fine.
Mr M.'s secretary: The Monday? (Yes) Oh, that's lovely. That's Monday, Monday the second of December. (Yes) Right? Monday the second of December then. Mm-mm. At what time?
Mr. S.'s secretary: Erm ... (Have you ...) ten, ten o'clock in the morning (Mm-mm) will be fine.
Mr M.'s secretary: Oh great. Right. Ten o'clock in the morning (Yes), on December the second. Now where should Mr Martin meet Mr Seshimo?
Mr S.'s secretary: Erm, I was just wondering if he could meet Mr Seshimo in my office and travel out er to the factory er together.
Mr M.'s secretary: Oh I see. You where ... er ... your office is in the centre of Tokyo, is it?
Mr S.'s secretary: Yes.
Mr M.'s secretary: Yes it must be. (Yes) Mm-mm. Right. Well. Let me just go over the

address. Now the address written here ...
that's a hundred ... now this is Ot, Ote ...
machi.

Mr S.'s secretary: Yes, that's right.

Mr M.'s secretary: Is that correct?

Mr S.'s secretary: Yes. One hundred
Otemachi.

Mr M.'s secretary: Otemachi? (Yes) Could you
spell that please?

Mr S.'s secretary: Yes. Erm. O-T-E-M-A-C-H-I.

Mr M.'s secretary: Uh-huh one hundred
Otemachi. Uh-huh great. At ten o'clock on
Monday the second of December. (Mm-mm)
Is that correct?

Mr S.'s secretary: Yes. That's right.

Mr M.'s secretary: Fine. I'll tell Mr Martin.
Thank you very very much for your help.

Mr S.'s secretary: Thank you very much. Bye
bye.

Mr M.'s secretary: Thank you. Bye.

Key language

Function: Arranging the time and date for a meeting.

Lexis:	*days of the week*	to visit
	alphabet	to travel
	secretary	factory
	boss	office
	speaking	centre
	conference	address

Structures: Could I speak to ...?
This is ...
What can I do for you?
the (first) week in (December)
He is coming for ...
He would like to ...
When would it suit you?
(It) will be running from ... to ...
... will be fine
the (second) of (December) / 2nd December
At what time?
(ten) o'clock in the (morning) / 10 a.m.
Where should ... meet ...?
Could you spell ... please?

PROCEDURE

Before listening

This unit could usefully follow earlier work on telephoning. A dialogue
frame for making an appointment can be built up on the board. For example:

Receptionist: Hello. This is the Summerville Health Centre. Can I help
you?

Patient: Yes. I'd like to speak to Dr Hewes' receptionist please.

Receptionist: Yes, speaking.

Patient: This is ...
Receptionist: Hello. What can I do for you?
Patient: I would like to make an appointment to see the doctor.
Receptionist: Yes. Would Friday morning suit you?
Patient: Friday morning is OK. At what time?
Receptionist: Would 9.30 suit you?
Patient: Yes, that'll be fine.
Receptionist: What's your name again please?
Patient: ...
Receptionist: Could you spell that please?
Patient: ...
Receptionist: Thank you. Dr Hewes will see you at 9.30 on Friday.

This dialogue frame could be practised in pairs, with students sitting back to back to simulate a real telephone call. The dialogue could be varied by imagining that the patient has a very full schedule or is being difficult. Let students suggest ways the patient might respond to the receptionist's question, 'Would Friday morning suit you?', e.g. 'No, I'm busy on Friday', 'No, Friday is no good', 'No, I work on Fridays'.

The remaining structures and lexis should be dealt with quite rapidly.

Tell the students they are going to hear a telephone call between two secretaries. Play a short excerpt from the tape and ask them to guess the nationalities of the secretaries. The purpose is to give students time to get used to the idea of listening to English spoken with a foreign accent before having to listen for any specific information. The English secretary on the tape conveys all the information necessary to the completion of the task and so very little attention need be paid to the content of the Japanese secretary's part.

Have photographs of two secretaries and introduce them as Mr Martin's and Mr Seshimo's secretaries. Tell them that Mr Martin is going to Japan for a conference and wants to visit Mr Seshimo's factory while he is there. His secretary is arranging this on the phone. Ask students to suggest the details she has to arrange. Read the memo on page 14 in the Student's Book. Make sure everyone knows that it is from Mr Martin's secretary and knows which details to listen for. This is an important step in directing students to listen for specific information while disregarding redundant information.

Listening task

Students have to listen for the day, date and time of the meeting and the address of the Tokyo office. If students are finding it difficult to sift out this information, direct their listening by asking for one of these pieces of information. Play the tape, ask for suggestions and fill in the correct answer. Play the tape as many times as is necessary for the students to complete the task.

Reading task

Ask students to say who they have to arrange meetings with, e.g. colleagues, friends. Encourage them to think about the types of messages they have to send and receive.

Look at the messages on page 15 in the Student's Book. Give students time to read all three and to underline words and phrases they do not understand. Together, look at each of the three pieces and decide where it would be found. Help students use context as the first way of determining the meaning of an underlined word. Often there will be one student who has come across it before. If not, use a good English–English dictionary. Finally, get students to circle the time and place of the meeting in each message. Ensure that the prepositions are also encircled.

Writing task

Depending on the ability of your students, you may choose to do the writing as a group or individual exercise. There is sufficient information in the three messages to construct a suitable answer to the writing task.

COMPLETED LISTENING TASK

7 Arranging a business meeting

Fill in the missing information.

MARTIN SERVICES

MEMO

To _Mr. Martin_   Date _Nov. 1st_

Called Mr. Seshimo's office
(Japan) today. Mr. Seshimo
will meet you on _MONDAY_,
2nd December at _10a.m._.
Wants to meet in central
Tokyo office, address
_100_, _OTEMACHI_

Alison   11.30 a.m.

NOTICES

URGENT

THERE WILL BE A MEETING IN ROOM 20 AT 1 P.M. TODAY FOR EVERYONE WHO WANTS TO PLAY FOOTBALL ON SATURDAY. DON'T FORGET

Wed. 2.30

John,
Came by but you were out! Do you want a lift tonight? I'll meet you at Jane's place at 7 p.m. Don't be late!

Elaine

LETTERS

It will be Anne's birthday on Friday 7th October. Come and help us celebrate.

107 Pine Avenue at 8 p.m.

Juan

Write a brief message to a friend arranging an urgent meeting. Remember to say when and where.

Tuesday 9 a.m.

URGENT!

Lucy,
Fran's birthday is tomorrow not Friday. Come tonight and help us plan a party for her. We will be meeting at my place, 3 The Avenue at 7 o'clock. Don't be late! Bye for now,
        Simon.

8 Shopping in an open-air market

OBJECTIVES

1 To give students practice in getting information by overhearing a conversation.
2 To give students practice in following a typical shopkeeper–customer exchange.
3 To give students practice in asking about and ordering a variety of goods.

RECORDING

Tapescript

Length: 1 min. 20 sec.
Number of speakers: 2.
Setting: In a busy open-air market.

Stallholder: Morning madam, what can I get for you?
Customer: Oh, morning. Mushrooms please, have you any mushrooms?
Stallholder: Yes, the mushrooms are behind the melons.
Customer: Oh yes I see. Could I have half a pound, please?
Stallholder: Half a pound of mushrooms.
Customer: How much is that?
Stallholder: Right, there we are. That's 52p, please.
Customer: Mm-mm. Thank you. Er, now the melons. How how much are those melons?
Stallholder: Er they're £1.50, actually.
Customer: £1.50! No, thanks, too expensive.
Stallholder: Too expensive?
Customer: I see you've got eggs here. I've never seen eggs on a vegetable stall before.
Stallholder: Yeah, well it's er, you know, where I go and get me er greens the farmer there he does them. They're free range. (Oh?) Very nice.
Customer: I see. How much?
Stallholder: Er, 78p a dozen.
Customer: 78p. Yes, I'll have a dozen thanks.
Stallholder: Right, dozen eggs, there we are. Right, that's erm ...
Customer: Have you got any tomatoes?

Stallholder: Er ... they're on the right er behind the apples. Can you see them there?
Customer: Oh yes. How much are they?
Stallholder: 50p a pound.
Customer: Ah-huh. I'll have a pound thanks.
Stallholder: Mm-mm.
Customer: And what's in that basket up there?
Stallholder: Oh that's er that's garlic.
Customer: Oh, no thank you, no. My husband won't touch it.
Stallholder: Doesn't like it?
Customer: No, awful.
Stallholder: Oh, we have it in our cooking all the time.
Customer: Look. I'll have a lime please, I think. How much are they?
Stallholder: Right. 20p each today.
Customer: Yes please, I will have one.
Stallholder: 20p each. That's one lime.
Customer: That's all thanks.
Stallholder: Right, that's the lot. Er ... so, let's see. Fifty-two, twenty-eight, fifty ... that's er £2 exactly.
Customer: Fine, thank you. Here you are.
Stallholder: Right, thanks very much. See you again then.
Customer: Thank you, bye.
Stallholder: Bye.

Key language

Function: Asking about and ordering goods.

Lexis: *numbers 1–100*   a dozen
mushroom   tomato
behind   on the right
melon   apple
half a pound   basket
52p   up there
£1.50 (one pound fifty)   garlic
too expensive   lime
each   There we are
egg   That's all
vegetable stall

Structures: What can I get for you?
Have you any ...?
Could I have ...?
How much is/are ...?
They are ...
I'll have ...
That's (£2).

PROCEDURE

Before listening

There are three topics needing to be covered before listening. Use visual aids to introduce or revise the fruit and vegetable vocabulary. Follow this with work on quantities. Cover not only pounds, kilos but also 'a box of', 'a packet of', etc. Finally, show how these quantities are abbreviated in a written list.

Try to provide practice of the key function using situations relevant to your particular students. If your class is working in commerce, for example, simply introduce 'quantities' and 'list-writing' in the context of ordering office supplies. Make sure students understand the objectives of this unit by not restricting the topic to buying fruit and vegetables.

Ask students to look at the photograph on page 16 in the Student's Book. Look at the fruit and vegetables and name as many as possible. Is this fairly typical of the fruit and vegetable shops in their country? If not, make a list of common vegetables that are missing and provide the English names.

Listening task

This recording is of a female customer buying goods at a vegetable stall. It is important to notice that the shopping list on page 16 in the Student's

Book is the *student's* list and not the customer's. The task is to calculate the cost of the shopping on this list by listening to the conversation on the tape. Make sure students are aware of the positions of the stallholder and customer relative to the stall. They are in the same position as the student, i.e. in front of the stall.

There are two parts to this task: first, to fill in the missing information on the photograph. To do this, locate the five blank labels. Make a list on the board of the goods to be priced. Some vegetables are already priced on the photograph so use these to demonstrate how to write the answers, e.g. 52p/lb; second, use this information to calculate the cost of the shopping listed at the bottom of the page. You may wish to simplify the task by completing the first part as a group before going on to the second part.

Reading and writing tasks

In this section the idea of ordering goods is developed further. Ask students to think of ways of buying articles which do not involve going to the actual shop. Ordering by phone, by post using a catalogue, by post cutting out advertisements, or by television are some ways which may be mentioned.

On page 17 in the Student's Book there are order forms which have been taken from magazine advertising features. They each offer a different item and require differing amounts of information. On the board write 'computer, sweater, photocopier, travel brochure'. Ask students to label the forms. Choose one of these to focus on, depending on the topic area you wish to reinforce. The sweater form, for example, has a number of items to look at, such as typical abbreviations (e.g. p&p), clothes' sizes for men and women, block letters.

COMPLETED LISTENING TASK

8 Shopping in an open-air market

Fill in the prices of the fruit and vegetables.

PINEAPPLES 85 P

MUSHROOMS 52p ½lb

IMPORTED TOMATOES 50p lb

MELONS £1·50p

FREE RANGE SIZE 2 EGGS 78p doz.

LIMES 20p ea.

STRAWBERRIES 55 P

Calculate the cost of the shopping on the list.

SHOPPING LIST

½ lb tomatoes	25
1 doz. eggs	78
1 melon	1.50
1 pineapple	85
Total	£ 3.38

Choose two of the advertisements and order the goods for yourself.

To: Canon (UK) Ltd., FREEPOST, Waddon House, Stafford Road, Croydon CR9 9ES. Telephone: 01-680 7700. Telex: 884 838. Facsimile no: 01-681 3588.

I'd like to know more about Canon compact copiers – masters of Space, Time and Energy.

Name: *JACQUELINE WOOLGAR*

Position: *ACCOUNTANT*

Company: *M & M'S GARAGE*

Type of Business: *TYRE & BATTERY RETAIL*

Address: *850, WIMBORNE ROAD*
WIMBORNE, DORSET

Postcode *BH9 8PQ* Tel: *0202-89345*

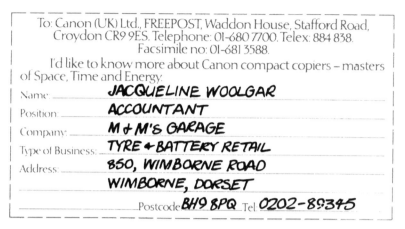

Take any NCL Caribbean cruise

FLY FREE IN AMERICA!

When you take any NCL 9 or 17-day fly/cruise, you can fly free on Pan Am to two more cities such as New York, Washington, New Orleans, Tampa, Orlando and Miami – and stay in the U.S. up to six months! Details in our brochure.

Prices from £765 per person include

- Return flights London Heathrow/Miami on Pan Am.
- Free Miami hotel your first night in America.
- Free cruises on all ships for children up to age 17 sharing with 2 full fare adults – 2 Jul to 11 Sept, 1983.
- All meals – up to 45 in a week.
- Jack Jones and other show business greats on the S/S Norway.
- All entertainment and live gambling at sea.
- A day on a private island in the Bahamas; plus other ports of call.
- Choice of 5 great ships and 6 great cruises.

Let your self go!

Norwegian Caribbean Lines
Clareville House, Oxendon Street, London SW1Y 4EL.
Please send your new full-colour brochure.

Name_____
Address_____

S/S NORWAY M/S STARWARD M/S SKYWARD M/S SOUTHWARD M/S SUNWARD II

Please send me by courier_____ BBC Model B Microcomputer(s) at £399 including VAT and delivery.

Cheque enclosed for £_____ payable to BBC Microcomputer System readers a/c or charge ACCESS ▱ BARCLAYCARD ▱

Signed_____
Name_____
Address_____

Postal Code_____ ✂

To: Scotcade Ltd., 33-34 High Street, Bridgnorth, Shropshire WV16 4HG

Please send me __*2*__ Icelandic Sweater(s)/Jumper(s) as indicated below at £26.90 (inc. £1.95 p&p) each.

LADIES' Qty. and size		MENS' Qty. and size	
10/12 ▱ (IL11)		33 ▱ (IM33)	
12/14 ☑ (IL13)		36 ▱ (IM36)	
16/18 ▱ (IL17)		39 ☑ (IM39)	
20 ▱ (IL20)		42 ▱ (IM42)	

I enclose cheque/postal order for £ *53.80* ~~or please debit my Access/American Express/Diners Club/Visa/Trustcard~~

No. _____

Signature *Jacqueline Woolgar.*

Name *JACQUELINE WOOLGAR*
BLOCK LETTERS PLEASE

Address *56, LAUREL ROAD, FERNDOWN*
DORSET Postcode *BH22 9AS*

VISA

Scotcade Limited. Registered Office: 33-34 High Street, Bridgnorth, Shropshire WV16 4HG. Registered No.: 1653140 England. Allow 21-28 days for delivery. Delivery subject to availability U.K. excl. Channel Islands.

9 Deciding where to eat

OBJECTIVES

1 To give students practice in following a conversation describing a restaurant.
2 To help students sort out the relevant information and identify the restaurant in question.
3 To give students practice in the language of arranging meetings.
4 To give students practice in reading some authentic material and writing a letter to arrange a meeting.

RECORDING

Tapescript

Length: 1 min 12 sec.
Number of speakers: 2.
Setting: In a street in the centre of town.

Helen: Hello Robin. How are you?
Robin: Hello Helen. What are you doing in town?
Helen: Oh, I've just come back from a fabulous holiday.
Robin: Oh yes, you've been abroad, haven't you?
Helen: Yes (Japan?) yes oh it was great. And you?
Robin: Well I'm not doing very much. I'm just doing a bit of shopping, really.
Helen: Mm. Have you got time to have lunch?
Robin: Well I think so yes. Oh wait a minute, not today.
Helen: Tomorrow?
Robin: Tomorrow would be fine, yes.
Helen: Right. Where shall we go?
Robin: Well have you any suggestions? I don't know the town very well for ... eating out.
Helen: Well there's a salad bar in George Street that's rather good.
Robin: In George Street. (Mm-mm) Yes.
Helen: Opposite the ABC cinema.

Robin: Mm. (Any good?) What kind of place is that?
Helen: Well they have one hot dish and you can have soup and a roll for about 50p.
Robin: That sounds good (Mm-mm) yes. And what sort of salads?
Helen: Oh a mixture for about a pound. Erm it's on the first floor.
Robin: So let me get this right. Where is it in George Street?
Helen: It's above the bookshop, on the first floor, opposite the ABC cinema.
Robin: Opposite the ABC (Mm-mm) first floor (Hm-mm) above a bookshop.
Helen: Yes. (Fine) Right. OK.
Robin: And erm where shall we meet?
Helen: Oh I should think upstairs, wouldn't you?
Robin: What time?
Helen: Erm, half past twelve suit you?
Robin: Yes, that'll be fine.
Helen: Good, look forward to seeing you. Bye.
Robin: OK. See you tomorrow. Bye.

Key language

Function: Describing a place and arranging a meeting.

Lexis: lunch   roll
         today   salad
         tomorrow   mixture
         salad bar   above
         opposite   bookshop
         cinema   on the first floor
         hot dish   upstairs
         soup

Structures: Have you got time to ...?
            Where shall we go?
            There's a ... in ...
            What kind of place is that?
            They have ...
            That sounds (good).
            What sort of ...?
            What time?
            (Would) ... suit you?

PROCEDURE

Before listening

Deciding what to do, whether it is where to eat, which television programme to watch, etc., depends on making suggestions and responding to these according to likes and dislikes, interests, needs, preferences and so on. The topic you choose to practise the key language is unimportant except in so far as it affects the lexis.

Role playing is a good way to practise the key language. In order to get a good role play it is important to work out a profile of likes/dislikes/preferences so there are some grounds for making a decision. The profiles can be constructed prior to the session or as part of the lesson. A profile might include the following information:
who: two friends, one a vegetarian
where: in the street
what: decide where to go for lunch today;   *or*

who: two business colleagues, one on a diet, other short of time
where: on the phone
what: decide where to have lunch tomorrow.

Use the photographs on page 18 of the Student's Book to teach the key lexis. There is a range of useful vocabulary displayed on the signs, so do

43

not restrict yourself to the key lexis. Encourage students to comment on the photographs, price, type of food, variety. Develop this into a discussion of favourite foods, favourite restaurants, diets and so on.

Ask students to choose one of these restaurants for lunch and give reasons for their choice.

Listening task

Ask students to listen to the tape for details of the restaurant where Helen and Robin decide to have lunch. Tell them to mark the corresponding photograph and note the words which brought them to this conclusion on a separate piece of paper. There is a considerable amount of information on this tape which is not part of the listening task. This is also the case in many other units and is intentional. The goal is to help students realise they can sort out the information essential to their needs and confidently disregard the rest.

Reading task

The Apollo theatre advertisement has been taken from a local paper. Its location is shown on the map. Give students time to look at page 19 in the Student's Book. Let them work together to sort out unknown vocabulary. Make sure they understand that the words in heavy type are the names of the groups, show or company.

Compare the shows at the Apollo theatre with those at a local theatre. Cover such aspects as seat prices and types of show.

Use the map to revise some simple prepositions of location.

Writing task

Students decide which of the shows at the Apollo they would like to take a friend to see. If none appeal, let them use an advertisement from their local paper and use those details. Ask them to think where they would meet beforehand and at what time.

Ask students to suggest points to include in their invitation and record these on the board. The degree of detail will be determined by the amount of guidance needed. When the writing task has been completed, students may be interested in each other's choices.

9 Deciding where to eat

Where did Robin and Helen arrange to meet? Put a tick in the box beside the correct photograph.

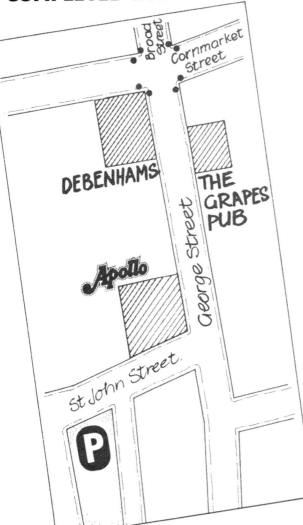

Invite a friend to the Apollo theatre. Remember to mention the date, what's on, where and when to meet.

Steve,

I have two tickets for the Hawkwind concert on Saturday March 17th. I'd love you to come with me. The concert is on at the Apollo, George Street, at 7·30. Let's meet in the Grapes Pub in George Street, opposite Debenhams, at 6·30. Phone me if you can't make it.

See you Saturday,
Jackie

10 Talking about holiday photographs

OBJECTIVES

1 To give students practice in following a series of connected descriptions.
2 To give students the opportunity to plan a holiday and choose the best location.

RECORDING

Tapescript

Length: 1 min. 40 sec.
Number of speakers: 2.
Setting: At home.

Steve: Have you seen our holiday snaps Fern?
Fern: No I haven't. (Oh they're great) I'd like to though.
Steve: Look. Here we are look. (Oh yes) That ... that's the train that took us there.
Fern: That's a really big train, isn't it?
Steve: Now what's special about this, you see this observation window here? (Oh yes) It's fabulous. You could all sit up here and see out from the top of the train.
Fern: Oh, have they got stairs in the train then?
Steve: Oh yes, yes (Well I'm blowed) Fully equipped. (Gosh) And here's the house we stayed in.
Fern: That looks nice.
Steve: It's fabulous. One of those wooden built cottages.
Fern: Yes that's really pretty. And look at that fabulous car in front.
Steve: Oh car! Typical massive, American car. (Mm) It was just lovely.
Fern: Yes, does look nice.
Steve: And here we are on a fishing trip.
Fern: Oh yes. And that was a big fish too.
Steve: Mm. Well that's Steve looking pretty pleased with himself.
Fern: Mm. Did you catch anything?

Steve: No, I was a disaster. (Ah) But it's really nice being out there.
Fern: Looks nice.
Steve: And then we went up to a ... camp on the lake. (Mm, yeah) Isn't that beautiful?
Fern: Certainly is.
Steve: Don't you love the way the trees come down to the edge of the ... lake there?
Fern: Looks really peaceful and lovely.
Steve: Oh it was so nice.
Fern: Are you having a ... meal there?
Steve: Yes that's right. That's us having one of our cook ups.
Fern: Mm, tent looks a bit small.
Steve: Well it was, but don't spend much time in the tent, do you?
Fern: I suppose not.
Steve: Here we are on the lake again. (Mm). This was a canoeing trip.
Fern: Yes, can ... do you know how to paddle?
Steve: Wasn't hard to ff ... to learn at all. Picked it up very quickly.
Fern: Well what worried me was you were wearing those life-jackets.
Steve: Yes, we all had to wear these silly life-jackets, but nobody minded very much. (No) It was really good fun. It was a great holiday.

Key language

Function: Describing and commenting on photographs.

Lexis:

holiday snaps	to catch
train	lake
observation window	tree
house	edge
wooden	meal
cottage	tent
car	canoe
massive	paddle
fishing trip	life-jacket
fish	

Structures: Here we are (...ing)
That's ...
Here's the ...
(That) looks nice / really peaceful and lovely.
That's/It's fabulous/really pretty.
Look at ...
It was just lovely/really good fun/a great holiday.
This was ...

PROCEDURE

Before listening

Most people like looking at photographs, so ask each student to bring in their favourite one. Use these pictures to practise the structures. Think of the exchange in three parts:

an introduction to the photograph: A: This is us at my sister's birthday party.

a comment: B: Looks really good fun.

a further comment: A: Yes, it was a great party.

Only positive comments appear on the tape. You may want to introduce some less enthusiastic comments too.

Some of the lexis may be covered while looking at the students' photographs.

Use the photographs on page 20 in the Student's Book to ensure all the key lexis is covered. Have students label the photographs if this helps retention. Do not let the key language restrict you if students are ready for further vocabulary building.

Look at the photographs on page 20 in the Student's Book. What can students deduce about the owner of these photographs? Ask them to guess the probable age, the interests, the nationality.

Listening task

Tell students that the man on the tape is showing five of his photographs to a woman. Their task is to identify these from the seven displayed on page 20 and to indicate their sequence by numbering them 1–5.

Reading task

Explain that a National Park is an area of land, often of outstanding beauty, which is protected from development for the use and recreation of the people. The American National Park system, with over 200 parks, is extensive.

Begin by looking at the items included under 'accommodations', 'facilities' and 'activities'. (*Note:* Accommodation is an uncountable noun in British English.) Ensure everyone understands the meaning of the black stars.

Writing task

Ask students to imagine they have won a contest and can visit the National Park of their choice. In order to choose the park, they should first decide on the kind of activities they would prefer. Then record the facilities and accommodation they would like to have available. At this point, use the chart of the National Park system to find the park which best fits the profile they have drawn up. Students could do this for themselves, or exchange books and do this for their neighbour. Finally, find out how many of the class would bump into each other on their holiday.

10 Talking about holiday photographs

Which five photographs was the man talking about? Put number 1 beside the first photograph described. Then number the other four photographs in sequence.

3

 (train)

1

5

4

2

COMPLETED WRITING TASK

You want to spend your holiday in a National Park. First, decide which activities you want to do. Then decide which facilities and accommodation you want. Now find the park which best suits you and complete the table.

NATIONAL PARK SYSTEM (*In or near the grounds.)	ACTIVITIES										FACILITIES							ACCOMMODATIONS				
	Boating	Fishing	Guided Tour	Hiking	Horseback Riding	Hunting	Mt. Climbing	Swimming	Water Sports	Winter Sports	Boat Rentals	Exhibits	Guide Service	Museum	Nature Trails	Picnic Area	Ski Trails	Cabins	Camp Ground	Hotel, Motel, Lodge	Medical Services	Restaurants
Abraham Lincoln Birthplace Nat'l Hist Site — Kentucky												★	★	★		★						
Acadia Nat'l Park — Maine	★	★	★	★	★			★	★	★	★	★		★	★	★	★	★				★
Adams Nat'l Hist Site — Massachusetts												★	★									
Agate Fossil Beds Nat'l Mon. — Nebraska		★		★								★		★								
Allegheny Portage R R Nat'l Hist Site — Pennsylvania			★	★								★	★	★		★						
Andrew Johnson Nat'l Hist Site — Tennessee			★									★	★	★								
Antietam Nat'l Battlefield & Cem. — Maryland		★	★	★								★				★						
Appomattox Court House Nat'l Hist Pk — Virginia			★	★								★				★						
Arches Nat'l Park — Utah			★	★	★							★			★	★	★		★			
Arlington House, Robert E. Lee Mem. — Virginia			★									★	★	★	★							
Arkansas Post Nat'l Mon. — Arkansas		★	★									★			★	★	★					
Assateague Island Nat'l Seashore — Maryland & Virginia	★	★	★	★		★		★				★			★				★			
Aztec Ruins Nat'l Mon. — New Mexico			★									★		★				★		★		★
Badlands Nat'l Mon. — South Dakota			★	★								★		★	★	★		★	★	★		★
Bandelier Nat'l Mon. — New Mexico		★	★	★								★		★	★	★		★	★	★		★
Bent's Old Fort Nat'l Hist Site — Colorado			★	★								★	★			★						
Big Bend Nat'l Park — Texas	★	★	★	★	★							★			★	★		★	★	★		★
Big Hole Nat'l Battlefield — Montana		★										★			★	★						
Black Canyon of the Gunnison — Colorado		★	★	★						★		★			★	★			★			★
Blue Ridge Parkway — Virginia & North Carolina		★	★	★	★							★		★	★	★		★	★	★		★
Booker T Washington Nat'l Mon. — Virginia			★	★								★	★	★	★	★						
Brices Cross Roads Nat'l Battlefield Site — Mississippi																★						
Bryce Canyon Nat'l Park — Utah		★	★	★	★							★	★	★	★	★		★	★	★	★	★
Buck Is. Reef Nat'l Mon. — Virgin Islands	★	★		★				★	★			★			★	★						
Cabrillo Nat'l Mon. — California		★										★		★		★						
Canyon de Chelly Nat'l Mon. — Arizona			★	★	★							★	★	★		★			★	★	★	★
Canyonlands Nat'l Park — Utah	★	★	★	★											★	★		★				
Cape Cod Nat'l Seashore — Massachusetts	★	★	★	★	★	★		★	★			★			★	★					★	★
Cape Hatteras Nat'l Seashore — North Carolina	★	★	★	★		★		★	★			★		★	★	★		★				★
Capitol Reef Nat'l Park — Utah			★	★								★	★	★	★	★		★	★			
Capulin Mt. Nat'l Mon. — New Mexico			★									★		★								
Carlsbad Caverns Nat'l Park — New Mexico			★	★	★							★	★	★	★							★
Casa Grande Nat'l Mon. — Arizona			★	★								★	★	★	★	★						

Activities	Facilities	Accommodation	Name of park	State
Fishing Hiking Horseback riding	Guide service Nature trails	Cabin Restaurants	Bryce Canyon	Utah

11 Making a drink

OBJECTIVES

1 To help students follow a sequence of instructions.
2 To give students practice in listening to expressions of quantity.
3 To give students practice in reading a variety of instructions and writing their own instructions.

RECORDING

Tapescript

Length: 1 min. 36 sec.
Number of speakers: 2.
Setting: At home.

Fern: Hello, Steve. How nice to see you. Come in.
Steve: Hello Fern.
Fern: You look awfully hot.
Steve: Oh, I am.
Fern: Would you like a drink?
Steve: Oh, I'd love a drink. What have you got?
Fern: Well anything you like, you tell me.
Steve: Mm. What I'd really like is a banana egg nog.
Fern: A banana egg nog! What on earth's that?
Steve: It's just like a milk shake.
Fern: OK. You tell me what to do and I'll try and make it for you.
Steve: All you need is a banana, some milk (Mm) an egg and some sugar.
Fern: I've got all of those.
Steve: Have you got a blender?
Fern: Yes, I've got a blender too.
Steve: That's fine then.
Fern: OK. What do I do first?
Steve: Now you chop the banana into the blender.
Fern: Mm-mm. There you are.
Steve: Add in half a pint of milk.

Fern: Half a pint ... OK.
Steve: That's about it. Now crack the egg into that.
Fern: Yes. That looks all right. Funny actually.
Steve: And then you just put in two small spoons of sugar.
Fern: One, two.
Steve: There you are. Just whip that up.
Fern: Right ... Mm, got a nice head on it!
Steve: That looks good.
Fern: I'll pour it out for you. How about that?
Steve: That tastes smashing.

Key language

Function: Giving instructions.

Lexis:

banana	half a pint of
milk shake	to crack
some	to put in
milk	(two) spoons of
egg	to whip
sugar	to pour
blender	Come in
to chop	There you are
to add	

Structures: (You/that) look(s) (hot/good).
Would you like ...?
I'd love ...
I'd really like ...
What on earth's that?
It's like a ...
Tell me what to do.
All you need is ...
Have you got ...?
What do I do first?
Now, (you) crack/chop ...

PROCEDURE

Before listening

This unit can provide a good follow-up lesson to work done on countable
and uncountable nouns, and on giving instructions.

Use pictures to help students differentiate these two types of nouns. Be
sure to include some common irregular plurals (teeth, children) and some
uncountables which typically cause problems (furniture, news,
information).

Practise giving instructions in pairs. Revise the key structures for beginning
and finishing instructions e.g. 'First ...', 'there you are'. Remind the person
following the instructions to show understanding, or lack of it, e.g.
'Hm-mm', 'Fine', 'OK', 'I do what?' You want a dialogue not a
monologue.

Play the first part of the tape and ask questions to fix the context for
the listening task. Ask who is going to make the drink, how she feels
about making it and what the drink is. Encourage suggestions about how
the drink is made – given its name and its similarity to a milk shake. Use

the pictures on page 22 in the Student's Book to help in predicting the sequence of instructions. The drink is made in a 'blender'. This machine can be used to mix drinks.

Listening task

Make sure the instructions on page 22 in the Student's Book are understood. There are two parts to the listening task: first, circle the ingredients used; second, sequence the steps depicted. Look at the list of ingredients and check for unknown vocabulary. If you have followed the 'before listening' activities students will be able to anticipate the ingredients to be circled. You may want to demonstrate the rubric by circling 'banana'. Ask for descriptions of each picture to ensure they are obvious to everyone before playing the tape.

Simplify the task if necessary by completing the first part together. Then ask for only the first and last pictures to be identified.

Reading task

Instructions for making three drinks have been taken from their packages. Some of the lexis will be familiar if the listening section has been completed. Make one of the drinks together if you think this will aid comprehension.

Writing task

Ask students to describe how to make their favourite drinks. If many of them are the same, compile the instructions on the board. If there is a variety, have students write their instructions individually and then choose a few to share with the whole class.

11 Making a drink

Circle the ingredients used in making the drink.

Cream ~~Milk~~ Butter ~~Egg~~ Orange juice ~~Banana~~ Water Ice cubes ~~Sugar~~

Look at the pictures showing the six steps for making the drink. Put 1 in the box beside the picture of the first step. Then number steps 2—6 in sequence.

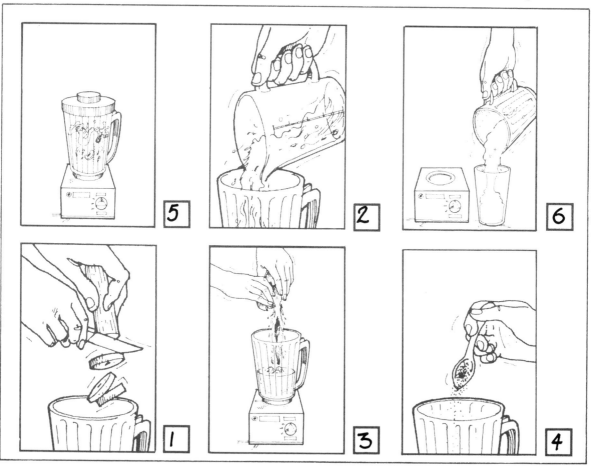

HERE'S HOW TO MAKE A RICH, COLOURFUL AND REFRESHING
CUP OF TEA:
— In a teapot
1. Fill the kettle with fresh water
2. Warm the teapot
3. Use one teabag per person. Add one for the pot if you like an
   especially strong cup of tea.
4. When the water boils pour immediately into the pot and stir the
   teabags round.
5. Allow the tea time to infuse — three to five minutes.
6. To each cup, add milk and sugar to taste.
— In a cup
1. Fill the kettle with fresh water.
2. Put one teabag into each cup.
3. When the water boils, pour immediately onto the teabags and stir round
4. Allow the tea time to infuse
5. Add milk and sugar to taste.

500 ml
Blackcurrant Health Drink

DILUTE TO TASTE

BEST BEFORE NOV '85

e250g
DIRECTIONS:
Sprinkle 3
heaped
teaspoonsful
of DRINKING
CHOCOLATE
onto a cup of
boiling milk
and stir.

Drinkin
Chocola

5 000128 040235

Write instructions for making your
favourite drink.

FRUIT PUNCH
Put some ice cubes in a
tall glass.
Fill the glass with orange juice,
pineapple juice and grapefruit
juice.
Add a slice of orange.
Stir.

12   Choosing from a menu

OBJECTIVES

1 To give students practice in listening to two foreigners using English as a lingua franca.
2 To give students practice in reading a menu and making selections for a number of diners.

RECORDING

Tapescript

Length: 50 sec.
Number of speakers: 2 (1 French speaker, 1 Spanish speaker).
Setting: In a restaurant in France.

French-speaking waiter: Bonjour monsieur. Que désirez-vous?
Spanish-speaking customer: Buenos días. Yo no entiendo francés.
Waiter: Bonjour monsieur. *Que désirez-vous?*
Customer: Er do you speak English?
Waiter: Yes, a little bit.
Customer: Erm, you know, I don't understand the menu. Er, what would you recommend?
Waiter: Oh I see. I suggest that you should have today's special.
Customer: And what's that?
Waiter: It's chicken with red wine, mushroom, onion and garlic.

Customer: It's chicken with red ... er with wine?
Waiter: Yes, red wine, mushroom, onion and garlic. It's very good.
Customer: Oh it sounds delicious.
Waiter: Yes, very nice, very.
Customer: Erm, what er could you recommend to drink?
Waiter: Er *le Beaujolais* is a red wine, house wine, is very good (Mm) for this kind of menu (Mm) very good.
Customer: Mm I see. I'll try.
Waiter: Thanks very much sir.
Customer: Thank you.

Key language

Function: Asking for help with a foreign menu.

Lexis: menu   mushroom
today's special   onion
chicken   garlic
red wine   to drink

Structures: Do you speak (English)?
Yes, a little bit.
I don't understand ...
What would you recommend?
What's that?
It sounds (delicious).
I'll try (it).

PROCEDURE

Before listening

Use the pictures in the Student's Book on page 24 to practise the lexis. If
you have a multi-national class, ask students to bring a food typical of
their country to class. In England a good delicatessen often stocks foods
from a large variety of countries. Have a tasting session and practise the
key structures.

The recording has a staccato quality typical of foreigners speaking
English together. 'Garlic' also proves to be a pronunciation problem fo the
waiter! A native English speaker would certainly provide a better model
for oral practice. However, this recording is intended to simulate the
exchange two foreigners might have when using English as a lingua
franca.

Students may be surprised to hear languages other than English on the
tape. Use this difference to good advantage. Play the tape and ask simple
questions, e.g. 'How many languages are being spoken?' 'Which languages
are they?' 'Why do the two men speak English?' 'Where are they?'

Listening task

Look at the pictures on page 24 in the Student's Book. The task is to
indicate with a tick the picture of the meal chosen by the customer. Play
the tape as many times as necessary for everyone to make a choice.

Reading task

This menu includes numerous vocabulary items which are probably unfamiliar to your students. Before turning to the dictionary, ask questions about
the form of the menu, e.g. 'What is the name of the restaurant?' 'Why are
there three sections on the menu?' 'Are the prices expensive/cheap?' 'What
do you think VAT 15% means?' This will demonstrate to the students that
they already know a lot about this menu.

Encourage students to use an English–English dictionary when they come
to look up unfamiliar words.

Oral practice of the key language can follow. Pairs of students make up a dialogue similar to the taped conversation between the waiter and diner. The 'waiter' recommends any dish and uses the description on the menu to explain what it is.

The situation used in this unit is just one of many where English is used as the lingua franca. Ask students to tell of other occasions where they have had to, or anticipate having to use English in this way.

Writing task

The writing task is an aid to comprehension of the reading. Ensure everyone understands 'Vegetarian'. Ask students to find a first course on the menu which a vegetarian could eat. The 'Vegetarian's Choice' can be filled in accordingly. Repeat for the main and dessert courses.

Either continue with 'My Choice' or make up further selections for other assorted diners, e.g. one who likes fish, one who only wants a snack. This could provide a useful homework activity.

12 Choosing from a menu

What did the customer order? Put a tick in the box beside the correct picture.

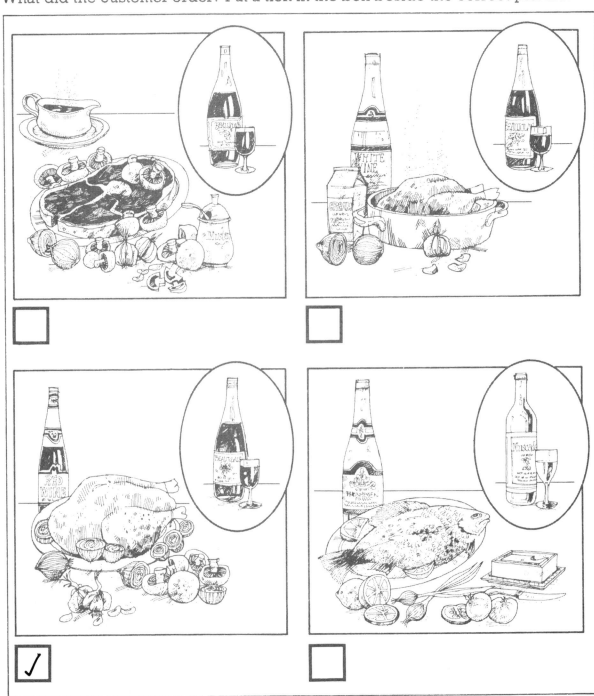

COMPLETED WRITING TASK

Write down the choice available to a vegetarian at this restaurant.
What would your choice be?

INN
on the
STRAND

MENU

All prices include VAT (15%)

Service is up to you!

Homemade Vegetable Soup with garlic or brown bread	90p
Original Recipe Paté meaty and delicious, served with hot toast and salad	1.05
Smoked Trout Paté served with hot toast and salad	1.05

———— oOo ————

Caribbean Tunny Salad tuna fish salad served in avocado with a mild curry dressing	2.25
Jacket Potato with Cream & Mushroom sauce with salad	1.75
Grilled Local Trout served with jacket potato & salad	3.25
Mexican Pork & Chilli Casserole served with jacket potato and salad	3.50

———— oOo ————

Yogourt with honey & walnuts	55p
Real Fruit Sorbets — orange, lemon & pineapple	1.10

Please see blackboard for any specials

Vegetarian's Choice

HOMEMADE VEGETABLE SOUP

———— oOo ————

JACKET POTATO WITH CREAM + MUSHROOM SAUCE WITH SALAD

———— oOo ————

YOGOURT WITH HONEY & WALNUTS

or

REAL FRUIT SORBET - ORANGE LEMON & PINEAPPLE

My Choice

HOMEMADE VEGETABLE SOUP

———— oOo ————

CARIBBEAN TUNNY SALAD

———— oOo ————

PINEAPPLE SORBET

25

13 Finding a garage

OBJECTIVES

---

1 To give students practice in following simple road directions.
2 To give students practice in sifting through excerpts from a motoring information booklet.

RECORDING

Tapescript

Length: 1 min. 52 sec.
Number of speakers: 2 (1 French speaker).
Setting: Driver stops passer-by in the street.

Driver: Excuse me.
Passer-by: Yes?
Driver: Do you know where I can find a garage please?
Passer-by: You want a garage?
Driver: Yes please.
Passer-by: Oh I think there's one just ... you'll find a garage just up the road. Erm do you want petrol?
Driver: No. There is something wrong with my brakes.
Passer-by: Oh got something wrong with the brakes. Erm well you really need a specialist garage. What kind of car is it?
Driver: Alfa Romeo.
Passer-by: Oh nice! (Yes) Erm, but I don't think you'll find an Alfa Romeo garage anywhere near here ...
Driver: Oh ... Do you know where Lime Street is?
Passer-by: Lime Street? Oh yes you want to be the other side of the railway ...
Driver: Yes I think so.
Passer-by: Erm do you know how to get there? (No) Ah well you need to turn round here and go back to the traffic lights (Yes) and then go right at the traffic lights and you go down that road until you come to a level crossing.

Driver: What's that?
Passer-by: A level crossing? (Yes) Oh er you don't understand a level crossing? (No) It's where ... it's where the road goes over the railway.
Driver: Oh I see (OK) Yeah thanks.
Passer-by: Just across the level crossing there's a right turning. Now that's Lime Street. (Yes) And you go down that street and I th... there's some garages down there on the left. I think it's that one. (Oh) Are you sure you've got that?
Driver: No I'm sorry I didn't understand. Just after the level crossing you tell me ...?
Passer-by: Yes, look. You go back towards the lights from here (Yes) and you turn right at the traffic lights, then you go down that road until you come to the level crossing. (Ah OK). Go over the level crossing (Over? Yes) Take the first right after the level crossing and that's Lime Street. And the garage, I think it's the Alfa Romeo garage, is down there on the left.
Driver: On the left? (Yeah) Thank you very much sir.
Passer-by: OK. (Bye bye) Take it easy with those brakes!

Key language

Function: Asking for and following directions.

Lexis:

to find	road
garage	railway
petrol	street
brakes	(traffic) lights
specialist garage	turning

Structures:
Do you know where ... is?
You'll find ... (just up the road).
on the other side of (the railway)
There's something wrong with ...
Turn round/left at ... / right at ...
Go down/back to/over/right at ...
... until you come to ...
on the left/right
Take the first right ...

PROCEDURE

Before listening

Most of the key structures are used to tell someone how to get somewhere else. It is worth noting that in this unscripted recording the person giving directions uses both the imperative form, 'go down there', and the personal pronoun, as in '*you* go down the road'. Students should have practice in using both forms.

Begin teaching directions using a very simple map like the one below.

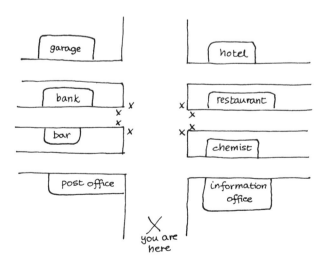

Have students practise in pairs asking for and giving directions to the places on the map. Remember to teach ways of opening and closing this kind of exchange. On the tape the person following the directions frequently signals his understanding by saying, 'Yes', 'OK'. This is a point worth introducing even in the early stages of language learning.

Ask students if they have ever driven in the UK. If any have had a break-down, encourage them to tell their anecdotes.

Tell them they are going to hear a conversation between a foreign car driver and an English passer-by. Play the tape and ask them to listen to find out the driver's problem. Open the Student's Book to page 26. Make sure everyone understands where the car is and which way it is facing. Remember cars are driven on the left in the UK. Also point out the railway line and traffic lights. The driver has a car handbook with addresses of Alfa Romeo garages in major cities in Europe. This is how he knows there is one in Lime Street.

Listening task

The task is to trace the route on the map and to mark the approximate position of the garage with a cross. Play the tape as frequently as is required for everyone to locate Lime Street and the garage.

Reading task

The information on page 27 of the Student's Book applies to British drivers going abroad. Be aware that this information might not be correct for your students travelling in Europe.

Make sure everyone understands the title of the booklet. Ask students to predict the kind of information it includes. Some of the more difficult phrases can be dealt with in this way before reading. Encourage students to help each other to understand the general meaning of each section. Aiming for the overall meaning is a better strategy than dissecting the message into individual words, looking them up in the dictionary and trying to reconstruct the meaning.

Writing task

The writing task asks students to make a list of things to do before leaving on a road trip to Greece via Yugoslavia. The 'Useful Information for Motoring Abroad' booklet on page 27 in the Student's Book contains a number of items that could be included on the list. First students should re-read the booklet looking for these items. Ask students to mark relevant passages either by underlining or making checkmarks in the margin. Second, students should select five items and list these in the space provided in their books.

COMPLETED LISTENING TASK

13 Finding a garage

Label Lime Street and mark the position of the garage with a cross.

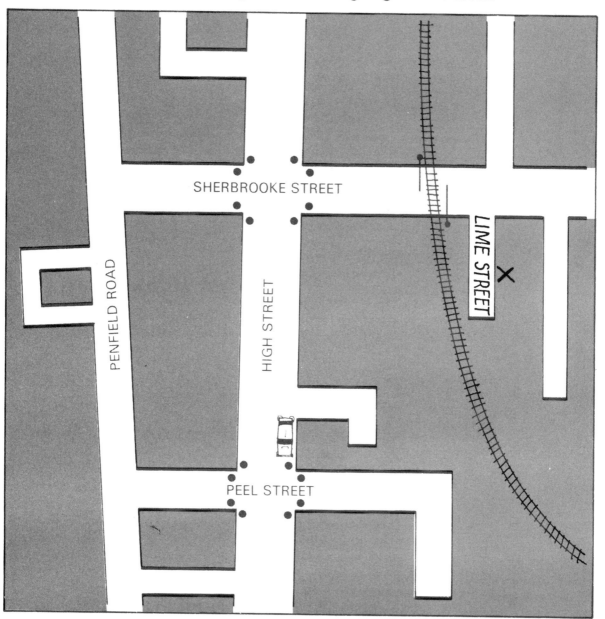

COMPLETED WRITING TASK

You are driving to Greece via Yugoslavia. Read the information below and make a note of things to remember to do.

Useful Information for Motoring Abroad

DO NOT TEMPT CAR THIEVES
LEAVE NOTHING OF VALUE IN YOUR CAR,
PARTICULARLY OVERNIGHT

Driving licence

An International Driving Permit is compulsory in Algeria, Austria, Bulgaria, Czechoslovakia, Greece, Hungary, Iceland, Morocco, Poland, Spain, Turkey and the USSR. It is strongly recommended for Finland, the German Democratic Republic and Tunisia.

Fire extinguishers

It is compulsory in Bulgaria and Greece (and recommended in Iceland) for all vehicles to be equipped with fire extinguishers.

First-aid kit

It is compulsory in Austria, Bulgaria, the German Democratic Republic, Greece, Poland and Yugoslavia (and recommended in Iceland) for all vehicles to be equipped with a first-aid kit.

Lights

It is compulsory in France, the German Democratic Republic, Norway, Poland, Spain, and Yugoslavia (and recommended in Iceland and Italy) to carry a spare set of vehicle bulbs.

Passengers

In some countries it is illegal for children under 12 to travel in the front seat of a vehicle — check.

Trip to Greece via Yugoslavia
THINGS TO DO:

1. Obtain an International Driving Permit.
2. Buy fire extinguisher and spare set of bulbs from AUTO-SHOP.
3. Put first-aid kit in the car.

14 Making enquiries in a department store

OBJECTIVES

1 To give students practice in overhearing people asking for and receiving information about location.
2 To acquaint students with a number of signs found in shops.
3 To help students find out about local rules and write a sign for one of them.

RECORDING

Tapescript

Length: 1 min. 40 sec.
Number of speakers: 4 (1 Japanese).
Setting: At an information desk in a department store.

Customer 1: Excuse me. I wonder if you could tell me where I could get tickets for Sunday's concert at the Forum.
Assistant at information desk: Yes certainly sir. It's er upstairs on the fourth floor and you go straight through the ... through the toy department. (Mm-mm yes) Very easy to find, you'll find the counter just there. They sell tickets for all the musical events in the city.
Customer 1: Fine. So I go up the stairs to the fourth floor. (Mm-mm) Through the toy department (Mm-mm) and I'll get the tickets there.
Assistant: Yes, that's right.
Customer 1: Well thanks very much indeed.

Assistant: Hello. Can I help you madam?
Customer 2: Er, excuse me. I've got a hairdryer and a radio which I brought with me from Japan (Mm-mm) but they don't work properly in England. Could you tell me where I can get something to make them work, please?
Assistant: Something to make them work? (Oh yes) I don't understand. Do you mean they're broken?
Customer 2: They are not broken. Erm I

think it's just for er different electrical system.
Assistant: Oh, you need a transformer. Yes. Why don't you try the electrical department, erm, where they ... they sell plugs and batteries and things like that. It's very easy to find. It's downstairs in the basement. (Mm-mm) You go along here to the escalator and straight down (Mm) OK?
Customer 2: Thank you very much indeed.
Assistant: It's a pleasure.
Customer 3: Could you tell me where the postcards are, please?
Assistant: Yes, certainly sir. They're on this floor, the stationery department.
Customer 3: Stationery department. Now where exactly is that because I've been walking around here I can't see anything any-where.
Assistant: Look they're very easy to find. It's just down there where they sell calendars, wrapping paper, ribbons and such (Calen-dars). It's on the end of the counter.
Customer 3: On the end of the counter?
Assistant: Yes (Right) That's right.
Customer 3: Thank you very much.

Key language

Function: Asking for information about location.

Lexis: to get (= to obtain)   plug
             ticket   battery
             concert   downstairs
             upstairs   in the basement
             toy   escalator
             department   postcard
             counter   stationery
             hairdryer   calendar
             radio   wrapping paper
             to work (*of machines*)   ribbon
             electrical

Structures: I wonder if you could tell me where ...?
                 on the (ground) floor
                 Go straight down/through ...
                 ... (is) very easy to (find)
                 Thanks/Thank you very much indeed.
                 Could you tell me where ...?

PROCEDURE

Before listening

Cut out pictures from magazines to use as visual aids to introduce or revise the key lexis.

Asking for and giving directions can be practised using the school building. Asking the whereabouts of the library, the fire escape or the coffee machine can be a useful exercise if this is done early in the term. Floor plans of the local museum, art gallery, etc., could be used for further role playing.

Ask students questions to encourage them to talk about overhearing, e.g. where it happens, whether it is ever useful/funny/dangerous. Set the scene for the tape by telling them to imagine they are waiting in a queue at an information desk in a department store. Tell them that the information desks are located on the ground floor near main entrances. This information is essential to completion of the task. Let them suggest the kinds of information they could expect to overhear. Alternatively, play a snippet of the tape and see if students can deduce the setting.

Listening task

Open the Student's Book to page 28. This is the student's shopping list. Tell them they are waiting to ask the assistant at the information desk where these articles are to be found. If they listen carefully to the conversations of the people in front of them in the queue, they will hear this information. The task is to note down on which floor each article is sold.

Reading task

Ask students to give examples of the kinds of signs they see when shopping. Tell students to look at the picture on page 29 in the Student's Book. A number of the shoppers are doing things forbidden by the signs. The task is to match the sign to the offender. Students can deduce the meaning of each of the signs by studying the picture and attaching the sign to the appropriate offender.

Writing task

Compile a list of rules which apply in the school, e.g. fire regulations, rules about smoking, noise, homework. Students may also have their own rules, e.g. for passengers riding in their car, friends borrowing their property. Ask students to choose a rule and write a sign for it. Stress that layout, clarity and brevity are all part of writing an effective sign.

COMPLETED LISTENING TASK

14 Making enquiries in a department store

Write down on which floor each article is sold.

Shopping List

Which floor?

Toy for Sara
(Music box? Teddy bear?) — 4 —

Birthday wrapping
paper — GROUND —

Postcards (6) — GROUND —

Battery for radio
(HP2 'D' size) — BASEMENT —

COMPLETED WRITING TASK

Match the signs with the people breaking the rules.

No smoking ① c

NO DOGS ALLOWED IN STORE! e ②

EXIT d ③

Washing aids
Soap powder

Paper goods

SHOPLIFTERS WILL BE PROSECUTED a ④

Please use basket provided! g ⑤

Find out any school or class rules that students should know about. Write a sign for one of them.

NO EATING, DRINKING OR SMOKING IN CLASSROOMS, PLEASE.

15 Making sense of a television interview

OBJECTIVES

---

1 To give students practice in deducing the topic of conversation, using only contextual clues.
2 To give students practice in reading a number of programme descriptions and detecting the main idea of each one.

RECORDING

Tapescript

Length: 1 min. 25 sec.
Number of speakers: 2.
Setting: An interview on television.

Interviewer: Are word processors easy to use?
Guest: Yes, they are. It's just like using a typewriter. (Hm-mm) The key board is just like a typewriter so in that way they are very easy, yes.
Interviewer: Erm, what do typists feel about them? Do they enjoy using them?
Guest: Well, yes. There are a lot of good things about them. Erm, ... for example, it produces things much quicker (Hm) than the typist could do. Erm, ... and it makes letters look better. You know, they they (Yes) look very beautiful.
Interviewer: But is there any reason now for a typist to learn to type er quickly and accurately?
Guest: Hm. (Does that take ...) Pro...probably less than (Hm) there used to be. Although of course, it does depend what kind of ... business you're working for (Hm-hm), really. Erm if you are working for a business where you've got a lot of the same kind of letters to do (Hm) then this machine would be really good for that.

Interviewer: If, if I were a secretary (Hm) I'm not sure I'd really like to have one, because erm everything is done for you, isn't it?
Guest: Yes, in one way. But then if you were a secretary you'd have much more time to do other things instead of being stuck behind a typewriter all day.
Interviewer: Gets rid of a lot of the routine (Yes) dreary part of (Yes, yes) the job. Are they expensive?
Guest: Well, no not really. Erm between about three and five thousand pounds.
Interviewer: Hm.

Key language

Function: Talking about advantages and disadvantages.

Lexis: typewriter   machine
typist   secretary
letter   expensive
to type   to get rid of
quickly   routine
business   to be stuck

Structures: (They are) easy to (use).
It's just like (a) ...
What do (typists) feel about ...?
Do they enjoy using ...?
There are a lot of good things about ...

PROCEDURE

Before listening

The approach to this unit differs from the majority of units in *Elementary Task Listening*. Generally, the emphasis has been to help students use their predictive skills to anticipate the frame and content of the recording. This is because in real life we usually approach situations with a purpose and some prior experience on which to draw. It is rare that we have to listen and make sense of something which comes straight out of the blue. An example of one of these rare occasions is when we catch a snippet of a television programme or radio interview. The question first asked is 'What are they talking about?'. The purpose of this unit is to give students the chance to listen to a piece of connected discourse and detect the main idea.

It is obviously important for students to be familiar with the key language but it would defeat the purpose if they came to the listening task with 'secretaries' uppermost in their minds. So revise the lexis of the context of occupations.

Listening task

Set the scene for the tape by asking students to imagine they have just turned on the television and an interview in English is being broadcast. The picture on page 30 in the Student's Book is the one on the screen. As you see, it gives little information about the topic of their conversation.

Tell students to listen to the tape and jot down any words they catch. Their task is to guess the subject of the interview. Collect the words together on the board and help students deduce the kind of machine they are talking about. Supply 'word processor' when it is demanded. If students have not caught any of the advantages and disadvantages of this machine, it is not important. Ask them to think about the changes the introduction of a word processor would make to the job of a secretary. Now play the tape again. It is probably better to move straight on to the reading and writing rather than dwell on the complexities of the language on the tape.

Reading task

The reading task requires the students to deduce the topic of each programme without becoming embroiled in subsidiary ideas. Detecting the main idea is a reading skill which can be developed through exposure to material which is above the usual reading level of your students. Direct students to read the descriptions of the three television programmes and to underline the parts they understand. Discourage the use of dictionaries and queries about individual words for the moment. Focus on what they do know. Encourage students to deduce the meaning of such words as 'home-maker' and 'bread-winner'. Take each programme description in turn and ask questions to help students understand the topic. Students will probably realise that the television interview they heard on the tape was part of the *Changes* programme.

Writing task

To complete the writing task, students should write a brief description of each of the three programmes. Show students how the key phrases underlined in the reading task can be used here. The writing task can be completed as a group exercise on the board if students feel uncertain about writing descriptions. The second part of the writing task is to choose a favourite television programme and write a brief description of it. This can also be simplified if necessary. Ask students to write the name of their choice and then the topic of the programme. They can compare their choices to find the class's most and least popular programmes. Do your students prefer programmes about science, crime, sport ...?

15 Making sense of a television interview

What were the two women talking about? Make a list of the important words which helped you reach this conclusion.

typewriter	business
typists	machine
letters	secretary
type	

COMPLETED WRITING TASK

BBC1
10.30
A Man's Place

It's a man's world, or is it? In this thirty-minute film, men talk about children, marriage, divorce, work and play. They tell how the changing role of women has affected their lifestyles and how they feel about it. What is a man's place in 1984? Home-maker or Bread-winner? Researcher is John Driscoll, camera operator, Nicole Garrison.

BBC2
10.30
Changes

This week we hear how the technological boom is affecting working conditions on the shop floor and in offices up and down the country. Interviews with factory workers in Leeds and with a woman who is introducing secretaries to the 'New Age' typewriter —the Word Processor.
EDITOR ALICE BROWN
PRODUCER ELIZABETH GLASS

ITV
10.30
Outlook

Outlook is back with a new series of reports to keep you up to date with all that's new in the world of entertainment. Stories range from the technical to the romantic, from stage to screen, from new releases to re-makes. There will be profiles of the stars of the moment the stars of the future and the stars of the past. The director with the right film script, the designer with the latest fashion, the musician with the hit song are all part of the new *Outlook*. The programme is introduced by Fran Levine.

'...And here's news of a remarkable technological breakthrough...'

Write one or two sentences to describe each programme: A Man's Place, Changes and Outlook.
What is your favourite programme? Write a brief description of it in the space provided.

Programme	Description
A Man's Place	Short film of men talking about their changing lifestyles in the 80's.
Changes	Programme about the way new technology is affecting working conditions.
Outlook	Report on what's new in the world of entertainment.
"Mystery!"	Series of ghost stories by famous authors.

16 Suggesting birthday presents

OBJECTIVES

1 To give students practice in listening to someone making suggestions.
2 To help students follow the responses to the suggestions and determine the favoured idea.
3 To give students practice in writing a letter to a friend suggesting a place to spend a holiday.

RECORDING

Tapescript

Length: 1 min. 18 sec.
Number of speakers: 2.
Setting: In the street in a busy town.

Alison: Hello Robin. What are you doing all alone in the city centre on a Saturday?
Robin: Oh hello Ali. Lovely to see you. Well, I am trying to do some shopping for Chris's birthday, (Mm-mm when is it?) which is tomorrow. Tomorrow.
Alison: Oh, not much time left.
Robin: No. I've left it rather late. And the trouble is I haven't any ideas at all. I've been thinking hard but ... no ideas.
Alison: What about some of those leg-warmers, you know like long socks?
Robin: No she's already got some of those.
Alison: Oh, well, that's no good then. Erm ... Why don't you go to the kitchen shop? You know it's just down the road. They've got some (Mm-mm) lovely things, an electric carving knife, they've got some ....
Robin: Electric carving knife? (Mm, for example) Yes ... the trouble is she's not really very keen on cooking. I think she'd prefer something more personal, really.
Alison: Ah, yes, OK. Well you, you could always try getting her some perfume in that case.

Robin: Hmm perfume's not a bad idea. It's rather expensive though and I ...
Alison: Yes true.
Robin: And I'm rather short of money at the moment.
Alison: Well how about a paperback? Chris loves reading doesn't she?
Robin: Now that's a very good idea. (Well good) I think I could go for that.
Alison: Good. There's a lovely shop just down there. See that sign? Just at the end of the road. (Ah yes) There's a bookshop round the corner.
Robin: Good, OK. I'll try that, Ali. Thanks for your help.
Alison: Good I hope you're successful.
Robin: Great to see you.
Alison: Good to see you.
Robin: Bye then.

Key language

Function: Making and responding to suggestions.

Lexis: shopping   cooking
birthday   perfume
idea   rather expensive
leg-warmers   paperback
long socks   [chocolates]
kitchen shop   [champagne]
electric carving knife

Structures: I haven't any ideas.
What about ...?
(She's) already got ...
That's no good.
Why don't you ...?
(She's) not very keen on (cooking).
You could always ...
(I'm) short of (money).
How about ...?
That's a (very good) idea.
Thanks for (your help).

PROCEDURE

Before listening

Give each pair of students a situation to work on together. These situations should have a part for someone to make suggestions in response to the other's problem, for example:
Student A is looking for a holiday job. Student B suggests a number of possible avenues to follow:
a) the local paper
b) the place where B works
c) an au pair position seen advertised in school
d) a new shop opening in town.
Or: Student A wants to learn English but does not know how to go about it. Student B makes suggestions:
a) ask English teacher at school about language schools in the UK
b) write to B's old school in England
c) work as an au pair in the US
d) get 'Teach Yourself English' books and tapes.
   Get students thinking about the difficulties of choosing birthday presents. Direct the discussion to ensure all the key language is covered. Open the Student's Book to page 32 and look at the six pictures. Use these to revise or introduce the key lexis.

Listening task

Tell students they are going to hear Alison helping Robin to decide on a birthday present. First, they should listen for Alison's suggestions and put a tick in the box beside the appropriate pictures. When they have ticked the four pictures, they should listen to Robin's responses to the suggestions. If he thinks it is a good suggestion, they should circle the picture. Then they should listen more carefully for the reasons Robin gives for turning down the first three suggestions and note these underneath. Approaching the task in these three steps is suggested because the degree of overlapping speech makes this conversation quite difficult to follow. Structure the listening so students are not unduly put off by this added, but natural, distraction.

Reading task

Set the scene for the reading by asking students to imagine they are studying in the UK for a year and cannot go home for the Christmas holidays. The advertisement has been sent by a friend who wants them to go on holiday together. Read the description of the two holidays and choose one. Have an atlas available so Torquay and Las Fuentes can be located.

Writing task

The task is to write a reply to the friend proposing one of the two holidays. Practise orally and show how the key structures can be used. The goal is to reinforce the work done in preparation for the listening. Whenever letter writing is the task, it is worth drawing students' attention to details of layout, even if this has been covered before.

COMPLETED LISTENING TASK

16 Suggesting birthday presents

Which four presents did Alison suggest? Put a tick in the box beside each correct picture.
Circle the present Robin decided to buy.
Why didn't he like the other suggestions? Make a note of his reasons beneath each picture.

Too expensive

Chris already has some.

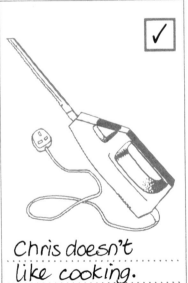

Chris doesn't like cooking.

SALE'S COACHES

91 High Street, Romford, Essex
Telephone (0708) 3221

CHRISTMAS IN SPAIN

(LAS FUENTES)
12 days, depart December 23, 1984, return on January 4, 1985.

Inclusive of luxury coach travel, Channel crossing, luxury self-catering apartment, ticket to New Year's Party (meal included)

£130 (minimum of 3 persons)
£195 each minimum of 2 persons

PLEASE ASK NOW FOR NEW 1985 SPANISH BROCHURE

CHRISTMAS IN TORQUAY

5 days, 4 nights — full board, depart December 24, return December 28.

Hotel with indoor swimming pool, games and keep-fit rooms, sauna and solarium.
£159 per person

NAME . . . .
ADDRESS . . . .
. . . .
. . . .

Your friend wants to know which of these holidays you would prefer.
Write your reply.

2 Wentworth Rd.,
York
November 12, 1984

Dear Sylvie,

Thanks for your letter. What a good idea to spend Christmas together. I think the Torquay holiday looks good. It's rather expensive but it will be fun! I'm not very keen on coach travel so the holiday in Spain is no good. What do you think about spending Christmas in Torquay?

Write soon so we can book early.
With love from,

Ingrid

17 Using a multi-storey car park

OBJECTIVES

1 To help students follow instructions.
2 To help students understand the range of instructions that typically accompany tasks in *Elementary Task Listening* and *Task Listening*.

RECORDING

Tapescript

Length: 1 min. 20 sec.
Number of speakers: 2.
Setting: Car driver stops passer-by on the street.

Driver: Excuse me.
Passer-by: Can I help you?
Driver: Yes. I wonder if you can tell me where the nearest car park is?
Passer-by: Erm, there's one just over there.
Driver: Oh lovely. Thank you.
Passer-by: Ah, but wait a minute. (Yes) It's rather a difficult one to use.
Driver: Why is that?
Passer-by: Well, when you go into it you have to take a ticket, (Yes) and this will raise the barrier. This will be a white ticket.
Driver: A white ticket, yes.
Passer-by: Yes and you keep the ticket with you.
Driver: That's all right.
Passer-by: And then you leave your car. When you return, you insert the white ticket into a machine ...
Driver: Where's that?
Passer-by: Just outside the car park. (Yes)

Just outside. Then the amount you have to pay will be displayed.
Driver: I see.
Passer-by: You put the coins in ...
Driver: Do I need a lot of coins?
Passer-by: No. No. You put the coins in and when you have put in the correct amount you will receive a blue ticket.
Driver: I see a blue ticket.
Passer-by: Yes a blue ticket. Then, you go back to your car and when you come out of the car park you insert the blue ticket into a machine near the exit and then the barrier will be raised.
Driver: Ah lovely. Well, thank you very much for warning me.
Passer-by: It's a pleasure.

Key language

Function: Giving a sequence of instructions.

Lexis:

(multi-storey) car park	machine
difficult	outside
to use	amount
to take	to pay
ticket	to be displayed
to raise	coin
barrier	to put in
white	to receive
to keep	blue
to leave	near
to insert	exit

Structures:

Can I help you?

I wonder if you can tell me where ... is?

When you ... you (have to) ...

And then you ...

When you have ... you will ...

PROCEDURE

Before listening

One way of covering the key language is to practise it within the context of following easier instructions. Students do not need to be able to manipulate the structures in order to complete the listening task. They need a receptive understanding.

Use the procedure for operating a drinks machine. Students will know the sequence of actions and may be able to express them using a variety of common verbs. Students need to become familiar with the vocabulary used in written and more formal instructions, e.g. insert, select, receive, display, raise.

Use the photographs on page 34 in the Student's Book to check students' receptive vocabulary.

By looking at the photographs students may be able to guess the task. Some may want to sequence the photographs before listening. While listening with a firm mental set is not desirable, encourage them to predict. Ask for the key words they expect to hear for each photograph. The photographs may spark off stories about the problems people have in multi-storey car parks, e.g. forgetting where the car is parked, losing the ticket, locking the keys in the car.

Listening task

Explain that the photographs represent the steps to be followed when using this car park. The students' task is to number them from 1 to 6

according to the woman's instructions. Give students time to look closely
at the photographs and make sure they notice that two different coloured
tickets are involved.

If necessary, the task can be simplified by asking students to identify
just the first and last photographs. Alternatively, identify the first two or
three photographs together. It always a good idea to spend time on the
pre-listening activities, to familiarise students with the key language.

Reading task

The list of instructions which appear on page 35 in the Student's Book
occur in *Elementary Task Listening* and *Task Listening*. They are also
fairly typical of instructions found in task-based examinations such as the
Oxford Preliminary Examination. Students should match the instructions
in the left-hand column to the tasks in the right-hand column. Having done
this they should be able to give an explanation of words such as 'sequence'
and 'label'.

Writing task

Seven instructions are listed but only six tasks are provided. Completion
of the reading task will indicate the missing task – g (Make a list ...). Students
often associate lists with shopping, so avoid lists of food items by getting
suggestions of items to include from the class. Point out that lists usually
have a distinctive format, i.e. written in a column with only very brief
details, often including abbreviations. Encourage the use of English–English
dictionaries to check spellings. Compare lists to see if anyone has included
anything amusing or novel.

17 Using a multi-storey car park

Indicate the correct order of the instructions by numbering the photographs 1—6.

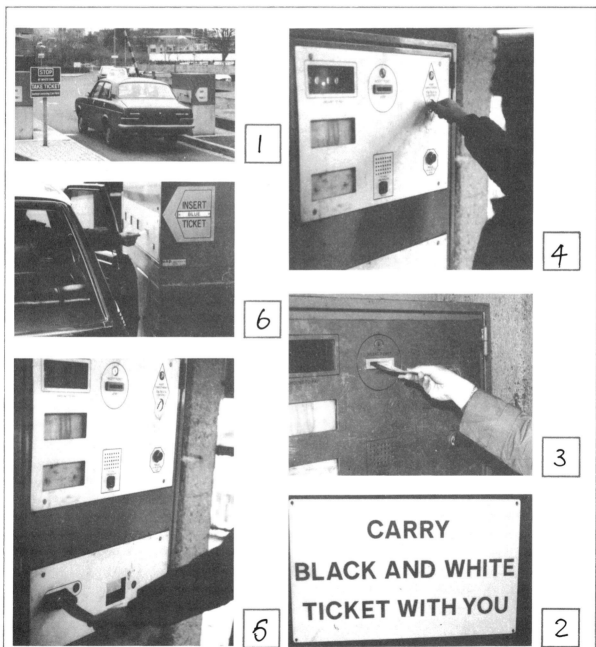

COMPLETED WRITING TASK

Match six of the instructions on the left with the completed tasks on the right.
For each pair, draw a line between the instruction and the task.
Read the seventh instruction and complete the task in the space provided.

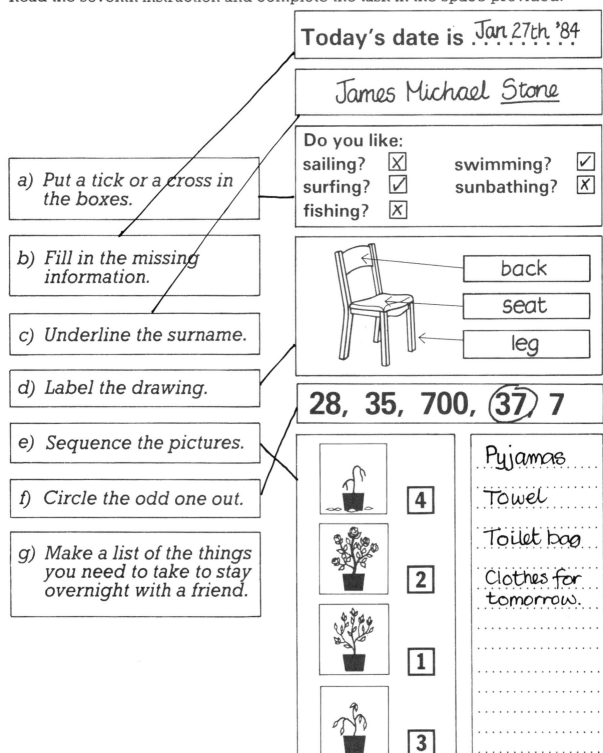

Today's date is *Jan 27th '84*

James Michael Stone

Do you like:
sailing? ☒   swimming? ☑
surfing? ☑   sunbathing? ☒
fishing? ☒

a) *Put a tick or a cross in the boxes.*

b) *Fill in the missing information.*

back

seat

leg

c) *Underline the surname.*

d) *Label the drawing.*

28, 35, 700, �37, 7

e) *Sequence the pictures.*

f) *Circle the odd one out.*

4

2

1

3

g) *Make a list of the things you need to take to stay overnight with a friend.*

Pyjamas
Towel
Toilet bag
Clothes for tomorrow.

18   Visiting the sights

OBJECTIVES

1 To give students practice in listening to a tourist asking for and receiving suggestions of places to visit.
2 To give students practice in following directions on a tourist map.
3 To give students practice in writing an informal letter recommending places to visit in their home town.

RECORDING

Tapescript

Length: 1 min. 49 sec.
Number of speakers: 2 (1 American, 1 Swiss-German).
Setting: At the check-out desk in an American Hotel.

Hotel receptionist: Good morning. Can I help you?
Visitor: Oh, good morning. Yes please. I'd like to have some information about er nice places er around here because I, I'm going to spend er the morning in this city and I don't know exactly where I could go.
Receptionist: Well you could go to the open-air market, it's not far from the hotel and they have de-delightful fresh fruits and vegetables, they have home-made jams and jellies, they also sell ceramics and hand-made leather goods. I think you'd enjoy it.
Visitor: Oh that's a good idea yes. Could you tell me where it is?
Receptionist: Yes. If you leave the hotel and you make a right turn and you follow a winding road, you go over a bridge, erm, onto Plum Island. And it's right there.
Visitor: Oh that sounds good thank you.
Receptionist: Yeah. There are also some tourist shops and cafés not far from the hotel erm if you are interested in buying souvenirs.
Visitor: Oh no I'm not so keen on that.

Don't you have something special which I should see?
Receptionist: Yes well, there's the cathedral. Erm, if you leave the hotel and make a left turn and go over the bridge you go up a hill and there it is. You can climb to the top and you have a very beautiful view of the city.
Visitor: Oh that sounds interesting. I'd love to go there. Is it far from here or ...?
Receptionist: No, no it's not far at all. Also don't forget the aquarium. We have a very nice aquarium here.
Visitor: What's that?
Receptionist: Oh aquarium erm is like a zoo for fish. They have large tanks filled with fish that you can look at.
Visitor: Mm well, no, not really I think.
Receptionist: OK. And there's also a very nice restaurant. Its called the Overlook and it's not far from the hotel. If you make a left turn when you leave the hotel it's right near, erm, and it overlooks the falls.
Visitor: Oh that's great. Thank you very much. That's very kind of you.

Receptionist: You're very welcome. I hope you enjoy your morning here.

Visitor: Bye bye then.
Receptionist: Bye.

Key language

Function: Giving and responding to suggestions.

Lexis: open-air market   hill
hotel   view (of the city)
winding (road)   aquarium
bridge   restaurant
tourist shop/café   to overlook
souvenir   falls
cathedral   far

Structures: Can I help you?
I'd like some information about ...
I'm going to spend ...
You could go to ...
That's a (good) idea.
Could you tell me where ...?
If you leave (the hotel) and make a left/right turn ...
Follow (the road) ...
Go up (a hill)/over (a bridge) ...
There is/are also ...
(I'm) not so keen on (that).
That sounds (interesting).
I hope you enjoy (your morning).

PROCEDURE

Before listening

When introducing structures for making suggestions, do not forget to teach ways to respond. On the tape the tourist responds enthusiastically to some suggestions, negatively to others.

The American receptionist talks about 'making left and right turns'. In British English it would be 'turning left or right'. The directions on the tape are fairly straightforward but worth practising before listening. Use the map on page 36 of the Student's Book to introduce or revise the key lexis.

Talk about the kinds of things students like to do when visiting a new town. Ask them how they would find out where to go if they were staying in a hotel. Look at the map on page 36 in the Student's Book and ask students to consider which of these places might be worth visiting.

Listening task

The task is to match the numbered places on the map with the names underneath. Tell students to listen first of all to the receptionist giving directions to the restaurant, market and cathedral. The only piece of information about the tourist shops and cafés is that they are not far from the hotel. The location of the aquarium can only be found by elimination. The picture shows the back of the hotel. So, a right turn out of the hotel brings you to 4, the tourist shops and cafés, whereas a left brings you to 5, the restaurant.

Reading task

Give students time to read the second page of the letter from Paul. Ask them to tell you what the letter is about and the kinds of suggestions their reply would include.

Draw students' attention to details of the layout of the letter, the address and date, position of the salutation, final greeting and signature. Students sometimes find it difficult to break the habit of putting their name above the address and beginning 'Dear Friend'. It is worth spending time on these two points and on teaching appropriate letter endings.

Writing task

Ask students to complete the reply to Paul's letter as if Paul were coming to visit them. Ask each of them in turn to read their letter out loud and ask the others to comment on the suggestions.

COMPLETED LISTENING TASK

18 Visiting the sights

Indicate the position of each of the places to visit by putting the correct number in the box.

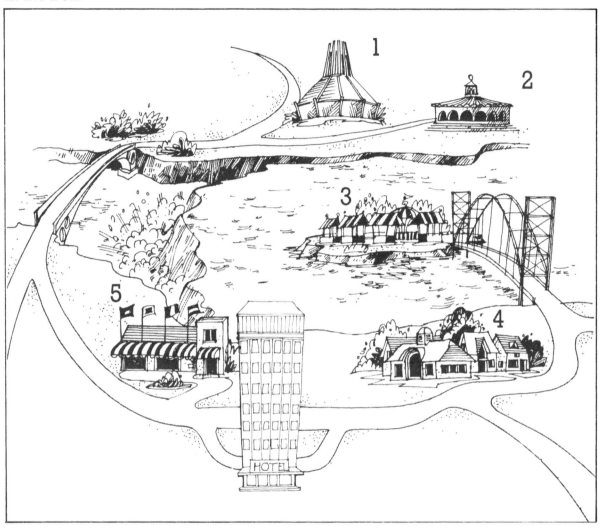

| 5 | Restaurant | 1 | Cathedral | 2 | Aquarium |
| 3 | Open-air market | 4 | Tourist shops and cafés |

COMPLETED WRITING TASK

Read Paul's letter to you. Use the information you have heard on the tape to help
you tell Paul about your city or country.

2
holiday. So I will be in
your part of the world in
July. Are there any nice
places to visit? I hope so!
I am looking forward
to hearing from you.
Best wishes,
Paul

1305, Colt Drive,
Portland,
Oregon 97202.

May 1st 1984

on this
ing,
ver on

Calle San Miguel 46

Barcelona 21

May 14th 1984

Dear Paul,

Thanks for your letter. There
are lots of places to visit in Barcelona.
You could go to the old city. I think
you'd enjoy it. There is a cathedral.
There are also several museums
and lots of good restaurants.

I hope you enjoy your stay here.
I am looking forward to
seeing you.
Best wishes
Jordi

19 Hiring a bike

OBJECTIVES

---

1 To give students practice in listening to someone making enquiries about hiring a bike.
2 To guide students to use the information they overhear to answer specific questions.
3 To give students practice in reading a brochure outlining rates for a variety of sporting activities and using this information to plan a personal schedule.

RECORDING

Tapescript

Length: 1 min. 18 sec.
Number of speakers: 2.
Setting: On the beach.

Customer: Good morning.
Shop owner: Good morning madam. Can I help you?
Customer: Well I hope so. Erm, someone up at the hotel suggested I came down here and ... arranged to hire some bikes from you.
Shop owner: Ah yes. A lot of people come down from the hotel (Yes?) It's very popular, yes.
Customer: Yes well, we're just on holiday here for a few days and erm they said it would be a good way of getting to see the island.
Shop owner: Well it certainly is. I mean you can go that much further on a push-bike or a motorised bike.
Customer: Ah so you've got two kinds of bikes, basically.
Shop owner: We've got two kinds but most people take the motorised because you can get around faster, you can also go on the beach if you like.

Customer: How old erm do you have to be to drive one of these things?
Shop owner: Ah there is a minimum age.
Customer: Yes, what's that?
Shop owner: Of sixteen.
Customer: Ah, yes ...
Shop owner: But that's only for the driver.
Customer: Ah-ha. So you can take passengers?
Shop owner: Certainly.
Customer: If I wanted to hire them tomorrow would there be any problem, can I just come along and get them tomorrow morning?
Shop owner: No problem at all. As you can see we've got hundreds here.
Customer: Yes it's true you have. And can I hire them just for the morning?
Shop owner: Ah that's unfortunately not possible. We only do hire for the whole day.
Customer: Ah, OK. So, erm, I'll probably see you first thing tomorrow morning, then.
Shop owner: Lovely.
Customer: Thanks a lot.
Shop owner: Be nice to see you then.

Key language

Function: Asking for and giving information.

Lexis:

to hire	driver
on holiday	passenger
push-bike	certainly
motorised bike	tomorrow morning
to get around	hundreds
on the beach	no problem
to drive	(the) whole (day)
minimum age	That's not possible

Structures: Can I help you?
(It's) a good way of/to ...
(We've) got (two) kinds of ...
You can ... you can also ...
How old do you have to be to ...?
Can I just (come along) and (get) ...

PROCEDURE

Before listening

Practise the key structures in the context of finding out the legal minimum age in different countries for such things as driving, voting, getting married, leaving school.

Point out the function of 'you' to refer to people in general. Extend students' abilities to respond to requests beyond 'Yes, you can' and 'No, ou can't'. Some of these occur in the recording.

Suggest to students that they want to hire a bike to see as much of the holiday island as possible. Ask them to make a list of things they would need to find out before hiring a bike. Their lists might include length of hire, types of bike, age restrictions and cost. Tell them to look at the bubbles in the picture on page 38 in the Student's Book and see the enquiries others might make.

Listening task

Tell students to imagine that they are on the beach looking at the bikes and overhear the woman's conversation. Ask them to note the answers to the questions in the bubbles. They should also note the answers to the enquiries on their own lists. Check the answers together. Find out which of the students' enquiries have not been answered. Rates will almost certainly be among them. Let students suggest ways they would ask for this information.

Reading task

Prepare students for reading and writing tasks using the situation on the tape. Encourage students to think about other activities which might be part of a holiday by the sea. As various water sports are mentioned, write these on the board. Illustrate each with a line drawing, if pictures are not available. Label the drawings. In this way most of the vocabulary items in the information leaflet can be covered before students even open their books. The meaning of the remaining vocabulary items can often be deduced from the context, e.g. free of charge, instruction.

Oral practice of the key language can follow. Show students how the questions on page 38 in the Student's Book and the information in the leaflet can be used to construct a dialogue about hiring a boat. Ask students to work on the dialogue in pairs.

Writing task

The writing task aims to further the comprehension of the reading. Individually, students decide how they would spend £50 at this sporting centre over a period of four days. The finished schedule must include an activity in each of the eight slots. Any of the £50 not allocated is non-returnable! If students enjoy these kinds of sports, the task should go well. If not, students should try to think of someone who would enjoy four days at the centre and plan the schedule with that person in mind.

The theme of this unit can be developed further. Use skiing holiday brochures to provide practice in scanning for details of cost, hire charges, lift prices, items included in total cost, availability of lessons.

19 Hiring a bike

Answer the questions by writing Yes or No in the space provided.

COMPLETED WRITING TASK

You are going to spend four days at the Beach Plum Inn Sporting Centre.
You have £50 to spend on equipment hire and instruction.
Plan your schedule for each day.

Beach Plum Inn Sporting Centre

Windsurfing

Board hire £4 per hour, with instruction £9 per hour. Instruction available for all levels. Boards must be returned by 8 p.m. Some boards for sale also.

Swimming

Two 50m. outdoor pools, free of charge to Inn guests. Lessons available on request (£3 per session).

Water-skiing

£7 per half hour inclusive of equipment and instruction.

Scuba diving

Boat leaves at 9 a.m., 1 p.m. daily. Trained divers always accompany party. £5 per half day plus £8 for equipment hire.

Boating

Canoes, rowing boats and sailing dinghies available for guests. All boats must be returned by 8 p.m. Lessons can be arranged (£6 per half hour).

White-water rafting

Day-long rafting trips available on Saturdays and Sundays only (8 a.m. departure). £16 inclusive of wetsuit, paddle, helmet and packed lunch.

	a.m.	p.m.
FRIDAY	Scuba diving £13	Swimming
SATURDAY	Windsurfing + lesson £9	Canoeing
SUNDAY	← White-Water Rafting → £16	
MONDAY	Water-skiing £7	Windsurfing £4

20 Asking about living abroad

OBJECTIVES

1 To give students practice in listening to someone asking about living in another country.
2 To give students a chance to compare the cost of living in their country and in the UK.

RECORDING

Tapescript

Length: 1 min. 30 sec.
Number of speakers: 2.
Setting: On the phone.

Jackie: Hello.
Helen: Hi, Jackie?
Jackie: Hm-mm.
Helen: It's Helen.
Jackie: Oh hi, Helen. How are you?
Helen: Hi. Fine. Look I had to phone you I've ju ... I've got that job in Montreal.
Jackie: Oh you haven't!
Helen: Yes, isn't it great?
Jackie: Oh, you lucky devil.
Helen: I know. I just heard, today.
Jackie: Oh that's terrific. When do you go?
Helen: Er, December.
Jackie: Hmm. Oh that's wonderful (Yes).
Helen: Listen, I wanted to ask you, because I know you were in Canada last year (Yeah?). Is it expensive there?
Jackie: Erm, what you mean living? (Yeah) No it's about the same as here really.
Helen: Is it? (Yeah, pretty much the same) Bu-but the salaries are higher, aren't they?
Jackie: Oh yeah. You get a much better salary over there.
Helen: Yeah. And what about accommodation? Is it easy to find?
Jackie: Erm, well we didn't have any trouble at all.

Helen: And, it sounds too good to be true actually, erm I'm going in December so wh-what about the weather. What will that be like?
Jackie: It will be freezing (Really?) So erm, let's think you should take ... er, have you got a really warm coat to take?
Helen: Yes, I've got my fur coat.
Jackie: Oh, fantastic. And some warm boots.
Helen: Yes.
Jackie: Take all your skiing stuff.
Helen: Yes I shall. What about the people, are they nice?
Jackie: Yeah, yeah. The people we met were really friendly.
Helen: Gosh I'm really looking forward to it.
Jackie: Oh I'm so envious.
Helen: I must stop now. I want to phone my mother and tell her the good news.
Jackie: Oh, OK.
Helen: See you next week probably.
Jackie: Well that'd be great. (OK) Let's get together.
Helen: Right.
Jackie: Bye then.
Helen: Bye.

Key language

Function: Making enquiries about living abroad.

Lexis: job   warm
        expensive   (fur) coat
        (cost of) living   to take
        here   boots
        salary   skiing stuff
        high(er)   people
        (over) there   nice
        accommodation   to meet
        to find   friendly
        weather   to look forward to
        freezing

Structures: (Is it) easy to (find?)
              What about ...?
              What will ... be like?
              It's about the same as (here).
              It's better (over there).
              It will be (freezing).
              We didn't have any trouble at all.

PROCEDURE

Before listening

Find one or two photographs of places which are markedly different from
the location of your school. For example, if you live in a city in a temperate
climate, find a picture of a desert in Arizona. Use the visual aid to stimulate
comparisons between the style of living 'here' and 'over there'. For further
practice of some of the key language, set up a role-playing situation.
Break the class into two groups. Let one be a group of mountain climbers
who are planning to climb Everest for the first time. The other group are
climbers recently returned from Everest. Have the first group prepare
questions to ask the second group. Meanwhile the second group prepares
an account of their expedition. There are a number of beautifully illustrated
books on mountain climbing which could be used to spark the imagination.
If this topic does not appeal, use any other where one group has to ask
questions of an 'experienced' group.
  Ask students to say what they would do if they were offered a job in
another country. Collate a list of the kinds of things which would influence
their decision. Ask them to imagine the job was in a country they knew
little about. How would they go about finding out about living there?
Direct this discussion to set the scene for the listening.

Listening task

The conversation takes place on the phone. Helen has got a job in Montreal and is asking Jackie about living there. Look at Helen's questions on page 40 in the Student's Book. Run through the questions to check students understand the task. Play the tape. Students should answer the questions by ticking the appropriate box.

Finally, ask students whether they would take a job in Montreal if one were offered.

Reading task

Ask students to look at page 41 in their books. These figures aim to give students an idea of the current range of salaries in a selection of occupations. Let students convert these figures into local currency to see where salaries are higher.

The 'Accommodation Offered' column has been included to give an idea of the cost of living. Prices would be considerably higher in central London. Ask students to underline the key information in each of the advertisements and then compare these prices with local rates.

Writing task

The writing task is to reply to a letter from the UK asking for information about living abroad. Ask students to imagine this person is coming out to work temporarily for a company in their country. Having completed the reading task on page 41 in the Student's Book, they will be able to suggest some points they would include in their reply. A letter frame has been included but you may choose to dispense with this and give your students freer rein over their writing. The letter reinforces the work done on comparatives. It also introduces 'but' and 'too'. Explain their use in the context of the salaries and the cost of living. To complete the letter, students cross out the alternatives which do not apply and fill in the name of their country.

COMPLETED LISTENING TASK

20 Asking about living abroad

Answer the questions by putting a tick in the correct box.
Fill in the missing information.

Ask Jackie about living in
Montreal – in December!

	YES	NO
COST OF LIVING		
Is it expensive?		✓
Are the salaries higher in Montreal?	✓	
ACCOMMODATION		
Is it easy to find?	✓	
PEOPLE		
Are they nice?	✓	
WEATHER		

Is there anything I should take
with me? WARM COAT, BOOTS,
. . . . . SKIING STUFF

Read the following information about living in Britain.

Gross weekly earnings of full-time employees in selected industries in 1981.

Great Britain £s

	Males		Females	
	Manual employees	Non-manual employees	Manual employees	Non-manual employees
Agriculture, forestry, and fishing	94·4	129·1	··	··
Mining and quarrying	154·5	195·1	··	105·5
Manufacturing				
Food, drink and tobacco	130·9	164·4	80·2	87·1
Engineering and allied industries	122·1	159·7	80·6	85·8
Chemicals, coal and petroleum products	135·9	181·7	79·7	98·4
Construction	120·9	152·0	··	80·1
Gas, electricity and water	143·1	178·6	··	101·9
Services				
Transport and communication	129·4	169·1	98·5	97·2
Insurance, banking and finance	126·7	184·3	··	93·7
Public administration	109·8	164·2	80·2	96·3

ACCOMMODATION OFFERED

Central Oxford. Bed-sittingroom adjoining well equipped kitchen. Suit professional person. £25.50 per week. Telephone: Oxford 379340 (evenings).

HOUSES TO LET

North Oxford. Modern 2-bedroom town house to let to careful tenants (non-smokers) until end of December 1985, or longer by arrangement. £180 per calendar month. Telephone: 01-670 1973 (after 19 October).

Headington. 1½ miles from city centre, close to schools and hospitals. Centrally heated house (4 bedrooms, 2 bathrooms) with attractive garden and rural views. Available 8 January to mid October 1985. £275 per month, including rates. Telephone: Oxford 723033.

FLAT TO LET

Iffley. Light, spacious, ground-floor flat: 2 bedrooms, bathroom, large living-room, kitchen; gas central heating. Available now. £217 per calendar month. No sharing. Telephone: Oxford 24463.

An English person is coming to work temporarily for a company in your country. Reply to his letter asking about life in your country.

Dear Peter,

Thank you for your letter. You will find living in ANTIGUA ~~very similar to~~ / very different from life in Britain.

First, the salaries here are ~~higher than~~ / lower than / ~~about the same as~~ in Britain.

(But) the cost of living is higher / ~~lower~~ / ~~about the same~~ (too).

You are coming in September, so it will be hot / ~~quite warm~~ / ~~cold~~ here.

You should bring some ~~warm~~ / cool clothes!

We are looking forward to meeting you in September.

Best wishes,

Frank Stone

21 Working out how to get downtown

OBJECTIVES

1 To give students practice in following directions given over the phone.
2 To give students practice in note taking.
3 To help students follow written directions and write their own.

RECORDING

Tapescript

Length: 2 min. 10 sec.
Number of speakers: 2 (1 American).
Setting: On the phone.

Bart: Hello.
Robin: Hello. Is that Bart?
Bart: Yes.
Robin: Bart it's er Robin here from England.
Bart: Robin! How are you?
Robin: I'm fine erm ...
Bart: Where are you? You're not in England, are you?
Robin: No, you're not going to believe this. I'm at the airport. I'm at your airport.
Bart: Oh, that's terrific.
Robin: Listen I tell you what happened. I suddenly got two weeks off (Yeah?) and I thought I'd just take you up on your your invitation to come over and here I am.
Bart: Absolutely. That's terrific.
Robin: Listen. Can I come and stay?
Bart: Of course, of course. (How do I get to you?) Listen er ... well that's the problem. I don't have a car (Oh) so you are going to have to get a bus or a subway or something.
Robin: Oh right, well that's that's no problem. Erm ...
Bart: Well, I'll, I'll tell you how to get here. Er ... the bus is really pretty easy (Yes). You're you're in the phone box in the main er airport terminal?
Robin: That's right, yes.

Bart: OK. If you look out ... er towards the road there, (Mm) there ... through the main doors. You go through the main doors (Yes) turn right (Yes) about twenty thirty yards there's a bus stop.
Robin: Oh I can see it through the window.
Bart: Yes, you get the bus it takes you right downtown (Mm) and when you get downtown at the terminal er ... you you change (Yes) onto another bus. A green one which is ...
Robin: Yes, er ... Listen Bart er ... I don't know about that I I think I might get lost if I have to change. I've never been in the US before you know.
Bart: OK.
Robin: Is there any other way I can get to you?
Bart: OK. OK. Actually the subway (Oh subway) is probably easier because it is more direct because (Yes) I could meet you erm at the stop right near my house. So er ... go out the main doors, (Mm) turn left. You go about 200 yards and then you come to a main road (Yes). Go straight over the main road.
Robin: Listen Bart ...
Bart: Carry on, carry straight ... yes?
Robin: Bart the only thing is, you know,

102

sorry to interrupt, but I've actually hurt my shoulder. This is one of the reasons I've got two weeks off, actually. I'm sure it is going to get better but I'm not really all that keen on walking a long way, you know.

Bart: Well, get a taxi.

Robin: Taxi.

Bart: Yes, a taxi. It's not too expensive. It's quick and convenient. The taxi rank's right outside the main doors.

Robin: Right, OK. That sounds great. Er … so I should be with you … I don't know how long the journey takes but I should be with you soon.

Bart: OK. About half an hour.

Robin: Oh great see you then.

Bart: OK. See you.

Robin: Bye.

Bart: Bye.

Key language

Function: Giving and responding to directions.

Lexis: airport	the US
to get to (*somewhere/someone*)	direct
car	to meet
bus	right near/outside
subway	quick
terminal	convenient
main airport terminal/doors/road	to hurt
yard	shoulder
(bus) stop	a long way
downtown	taxi
to change (*buses*)	taxi rank
to get lost	

Structures: Is that …?
It's (Robin) here.
I('ve) got (two weeks) off.
Can I (come) and (stay)?
I'll tell you how to (get here).
(You) go straight through … /over …
The (subway) is easier.
Turn left/right …
There's …
You come to …
(I'm) not keen on (walking).
It's not too (expensive).
That sounds (great).
It takes (half an hour).

PROCEDURE

Before listening

Use this unit after work on giving and following directions has been done. Focus on the second objective of this unit, which is to practise note taking. In real life the response of the listener to the directions given by Bart might be to jot down very brief details and stop when it becomes clear the directions are impracticable.

There are three aspects of note taking which you may want to cover: first of all, notes typically lack function words, e.g. pronouns, articles; secondly, the use of symbols to stand for some common relations, e.g. ∴ (therefore), = (equals/means), ↑ increasing/rising; thirdly, the use of common abbreviations, e.g. R (right), L (left), 1st (first), N, S (north, south), Tel. (telephone).

In this recording the traveller, Robin, has arrived in America to stay with his friend. He has arrived unexpectedly and so phones to find out how to get to his friend's house.

In addition to the preparation for note taking, students will probably need practice in interpreting the variety of responses to the suggestions. Ask students to suggest ways you might spend your evenings off. Respond using the structures and making your reaction to the suggestions quite clear.

Set the scene for the listening. Ask them to suggest the alternatives Bart will probably mention. Ask them to think about the advantages and disadvantages of these as seen from the point of view of a transatlantic traveller.

Listening task

Ask students to open their books to page 42 and to read the instructions. Make sure everyone realises that the subway sign is the circled letter T. This sign is used to indicate the stations of the Massachusetts Bay Transportation Authority in Boston. Subway signs vary from city to city in the US.

Then ask students to listen for the directions to the bus, subway and taxi rank and note these briefly in the appropriate space. This recording is more difficult than the others on the tape. This is largely due to the two speakers interrupting each other and the large amount of overlapping speech. The content is not particularly difficult. Play the tape as many times as is necessary.

Rather than take notes of the directions, some students may prefer to draw a map/diagram. This can show comprehension equally well.

Students should tick Robin's choice, and note his reasons in the 'Other information' column. Finally, ask them to note the reasons for not choosing the remaining methods of transport.

Reading task

This is adapted from an English games book and should be fun to do. The compass directions are not usually included in oral directions given in British English. However, they are common in American directions. The passage will reinforce earlier work on directions and also introduce new structures and vocabulary. Ask students to quickly follow the directions and say where they end up. Check students' whereabouts!

Writing task

Using the map on page 43, let each student write directions in note form for getting from one place to another. Check these and provide any new language required. Let students find out how effective their instructions are by asking their neighbour to follow them. If you would prefer to use this task for oral practice, ask students to read out their notes and have the whole class follow them.

21 Working out how to get downtown

Where are the buses, the subway and the taxis? Make a note of the directions that Bart gave Robin in the column beside each sign.
Which means of transport did Robin choose? Put a tick in the box beside the correct sign.
Why did he choose this means of transport and not the others? Make a note of his reasons in the second column.

	Directions	Other information
NO PARKING / BUS STOP	Out main doors, turn right, 20-30 yds → Bus stop.	Have to change buses.
T	Out main doors, turn left, 200 yds → main road, cross over	Too far to walk.
TAXI / NO PARKING / TAXI STAND ✓	Right outside main doors.	Not expensive, quick, convenient.

COMPLETED WRITING TASK

Trace the written directions on the map. Where do they take you?

Where are you going?

Walk north until you reach the post office and then turn left. Follow this road until you see the park sign on your right. Take the short cut through the park. When you leave the park, go north for a short distance. Take the first road on your left and there you are. You can't miss it!

The Cinema.

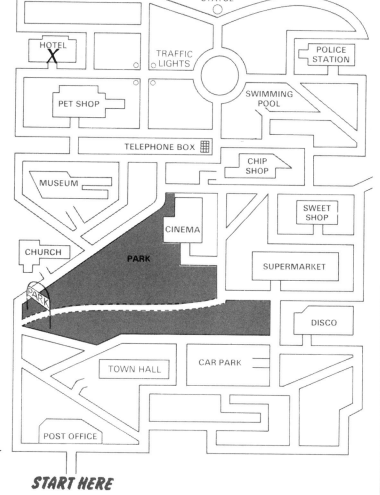

Write directions to another place on the map.
Use the directions above to help you.
Mark your starting point with a cross.

Leave the hotel and turn left. Follow this road until you reach a roundabout. Take the second exit and go east for a short distance.
It's a big building on your left. You can't miss it.